T0316572

Cambridge Elements ≡

Elements in Child Development
edited by
Marc H. Bornstein
National Institute of Child Health and Human Development, Bethesda
Institute for Fiscal Studies, London
UNICEF, New York City

THE NATURE OF INTELLIGENCE AND ITS DEVELOPMENT IN CHILDHOOD

Robert J. Sternberg
Cornell University

CAMBRIDGE
UNIVERSITY PRESS

CAMBRIDGE
UNIVERSITY PRESS

University Printing House, Cambridge CB2 8BS, United Kingdom

One Liberty Plaza, 20th Floor, New York, NY 10006, USA

477 Williamstown Road, Port Melbourne, VIC 3207, Australia

314–321, 3rd Floor, Plot 3, Splendor Forum, Jasola District Centre,
New Delhi – 110025, India

79 Anson Road, #06–04/06, Singapore 079906

Cambridge University Press is part of the University of Cambridge.

It furthers the University's mission by disseminating knowledge in the pursuit of
education, learning, and research at the highest international levels of excellence.

www.cambridge.org
Information on this title: www.cambridge.org/9781108791533
DOI: 10.1017/9781108866217

First published 2020

A catalogue record for this publication is available from the British Library.

ISBN 978-1-108-79153-3 Paperback
ISSN 2632-9948 (online)
ISSN 2632-993X (print)

The Nature of Intelligence and Its Development in Childhood

Elements in Child Development

DOI: 10.1017/9781108866217
First published online: November 2020

Robert J. Sternberg
Cornell University
Author for correspondence: robert.sternberg@cornell.edu

Abstract: In this Element, I first introduce intelligence in terms of historical definitions. I show that intelligence, as conceived even by the originators of the first intelligence tests, Alfred Binet and David Wechsler, is a much broader construct than just scores on narrow tests of intelligence and their proxies. I then review the major approaches to understanding intelligence and its development: the psychometric (test-based), cognitive and neurocognitive (intelligence as a set of brain-based cognitive representations and processes), systems, cultural, and developmental approaches. These approaches, taken together, present a much more complex portrait of intelligence and its development than the one that would be ascertained just from scores on intelligence tests. Finally, I draw some take-away conclusions.

Keywords: intelligence, child development, human abilities, individual differences, successful intelligence

ISBNs: 9781108791533 (PB), 9781108866217 (OC)
ISSNs: 2632-9948 (online), ISSN 2632-993X (print)

Contents

1 Introduction

The goal of this Element is to demonstrate that simplistic notions about intelligence, such as that intelligence is merely IQ or some general factor of intelligence, greatly simplify and distort our understanding of what intelligence is. Intelligence involves much more than IQ or scores on conventional standardized tests. By simplifying and packaging our notion of intelligence in terms of standardized tests, society does an injustice to many young people. Some young people may have a considerable or even an immense capacity to succeed in life but not succeed at IQ tests or their proxies, such as the SAT and ACT. (IQ proxies are tests that correlate highly with IQ tests but go by a different name and usually are marketed as serving a purpose other than that of measuring IQ.) At the same time, such tests may identify as high in potential young people whose ability to succeed in life, by any standard except IQ test performance, is much more limited.

In this Element, I first introduce intelligence in terms of historical definitions. I show that intelligence, as conceived even by the originators of the first intelligence tests, Alfred Binet and David Wechsler, is a much broader construct than just scores on narrow tests of intelligence and their proxies. I then review the major approaches to understanding intelligence and its development: the psychometric (test-based), cognitive and neurocognitive (intelligence as a set of brain-based cognitive representations and processes), systems, cultural, and developmental approaches. These approaches, taken together, present a much more complex portrait of intelligence and its development than the one that would be ascertained just from scores on intelligence tests. Finally, I draw some take-away conclusions.

This Element presents what I hope is a readable and brief overview for laypeople, students, and scholars who may not have much acquaintance with the field. It is intended to introduce the subject. Although it presents my own point of view, it presents many other points of view as well.

In the beginning and in the end, I believe that intelligence is about adaptation to the environment. Theories, research, and tests of intelligence should be evaluated in terms of the extent to which they can successfully account for how people adapt to their environments, and why some people adapt better than others. Intelligence tests have not done a very credible job of characterizing or even explaining intelligence as adaptation. Other approaches have done quite a bit better. This Element will provide readers with a chance to see all that other approaches have added.

2 Early Conceptions of Intelligence

2.1 Important Definitions of Intelligence

There have been many definitions of intelligence (Sternberg, 1990). However, I discuss here only a few of those of both historical and contemporary significance. In talking about intelligence, I will be talking not only about intelligence labeled as such, but also intelligence as given a variety of other labels, such as general mental ability (GMA), general intelligence (*g*), or scholastic aptitude (Frey & Detterman, 2004; Koenig, Frey, & Detterman, 2008; Sackett, Shewach, & Dahlke, 2019).

2.1.1 Alfred Binet and David Wechsler: Intelligence as Judgment and Ability to Adapt to the Environment

The most important historical definition is almost certainly that of Alfred Binet and Theodore Simon (1916, pp. 42–43):

> It seems to us that in intelligence there is a fundamental faculty, the alteration or the lack of which is of the utmost importance for practical life. This faculty is judgment, otherwise called good sense, practical sense, initiative, the faculty of adapting one's self to circumstances.

Alfred Binet was the "father" of intelligence testing as we know it today. Binet was a man of many talents: He was a researcher, he was a policy-maker, and he had a degree in law. In terms of practice (although not theory), he was the most eminent intelligence researcher of all time. Binet was concerned that children be placed into education that was appropriate to their abilities – that they not be shunted to special education because teachers found them to have behavioral problems or simply to be too difficult to teach for reasons unrelated to their intelligence. There are three important features to notice in Binet's definition.

The first feature of Binet's definition is that intelligence involves good judgment. It is not merely about solving tricky or even routine algebra or geometry problems or reading banal reading comprehension passages and answering questions about them. It is about making judgments in your life. For a child, how should one react to a bully? Should one always obey directions from a parent or teacher that one does not want to obey? Is a particular classmate a good friend or only trying to use you? For an adult, should one get married to a particular partner? Should one get divorced? Is the business deal one is about to make a good one or one that may lead you to ruin? Judgment is at the center of intelligence, not facts one memorizes for a test or trivial algebraic or geometric problems that one may or may not remember how to solve.

The second feature prominent in Binet's definition is that intelligence is about practical problems. It is not about arcane, trivial problems that no one would care about outside a testing situation. Somehow, societal notions about intelligence have become seriously distorted from the intentions of Binet, who created the first modern intelligence test. I believe Binet, were he alive today, would be horrified at the warped and distorted view of intelligence that has come to reign today as a result of a testing industry that long ago got out of control. The testing industry is not solely responsible: Many institutions – testing companies, of course, but also primary and secondary schools, high schools, test preparation companies, college admissions counselors, and others – collaborate. Children are forced to take tests that do not necessarily fully or accurately reflect their abilities or their accomplishments.

The third feature to notice is Binet's use of the term "initiative." Initiative is not a "cognitive" variable – it is not about how one thinks. Initiative is one's willingness to get things done and to take responsibility for them. It would seem to be more about how one uses one's intelligence rather than about the intelligence one has. Not according to Binet. Binet probably would not have viewed as particularly intelligent IQ test kings and queens who merely score in the top percentiles of IQ tests and proxy IQ tests, such as SATs and ACTs. He probably would not have been interested in whether one is a member of Mensa (requiring an IQ of roughly 130, in the top 2 percent of the population) or even of the Three Sigma Intelligence Society (for which membership requires an IQ of 145, which is in roughly the top 0.15 percent of the population). The reason is that one can have a high IQ but be utterly lacking in initiative, except perhaps to do well on IQ tests.

It's great to have a high IQ, but high IQ tells one little or nothing about a person's initiative: one's getting a job done properly that needs to be done and then taking responsibility for one's work, or one's not getting the job done properly and taking responsibility for not getting it done, or for doing it improperly. Binet was interested in what children actually could do inside and outside the classroom, not just in some abstract ability that would never see the light of day. Children not only need to have intellectual abilities for abstract thinking, they also need to have the initiative to put those abilities to use and make the most of them.

The fourth feature is that Binet's emphasis in his definition is on adapting oneself to circumstances – in other words, to the environment in which one lives. This characteristic was to prove to be more central to subsequent definitions of intelligence than was any other single characteristic. For example, in 1921, a series of experts wrote about what they believed intelligence to be, and nothing stood out more in common in those definitions than adaptation to the environment ("Intelligence and its measurement," 1921). For a child, adaptation can mean making the most of schooling or other educational opportunities, as well as social interaction opportunities through friendships, athletics, clubs, and the like.

What exactly does "adaptation to the environment" mean? It means that the cornerstone of intelligence is that life throws at us all many situations, expected and unexpected, and that intelligence is about our facility in handling these diverse situations. It is not about our ability to fill in bubbles on a multiple choice test or about our ability to outguess a tester regarding what they had in mind when they created a set of wily distractor (wrong) answers designed to sucker us into picking one of them. Intelligence is about what children or adults do when confronted with novel situations: what a child does when their new teacher seems to pick on them; or what we do when, for example, there is a pandemic and we've never experienced a pandemic before; or when we suddenly lose a job we have held for many years and have no back-up plan; or when we discover that someone we love has been having an affair and we feel like killing someone. In each case, do we adapt to the environment, or do we fail to adapt?

It is important to understand how Binet came to his definition. In early turn-of-the-20th-century France, Binet was asked by the French Ministry of Education in Paris to devise a test that would separate children who needed special help in school from those who may have been poor performers in school but not for reasons of lack of mental ability. For example, some children, as any parent or teacher knows, are just difficult. They may have behavioral issues, or they simply may not be interested in learning. Or they may have problems at home that they carry over into the classroom and that teachers may not even know exist.

The reason the Ministry thought the issue to be important is that if a child who is capable of learning is put into a class for slower learners, that child may never catch up to where they might otherwise have been. That is, one has a child who is learning slowly and, once the student is placed in a class for slow learners, predictions that the child will learn slowly often turn out to become a self-fulfilling prophecy. This kind of mistaken placement is as likely to happen today as it was in the early 20th century.

Why would children mistakenly be placed in classes that are a poor fit for them? There are several reasons. A first is that teachers might just not want the children in their classes. The kids were hard to teach – why not give the problem to someone else who perhaps is better trained to handle it? A second reason is that teachers do not always know about problems at home so may not have recognized home life as a source of poor performance. A third reason is that, in those days, there was no clear distinction between children living with a general intellectual disability and children living with a specific learning disability. So, teachers may have thought that a student with a specific learning disability simply was incapable of learning at a level commensurate with what the school expected. And a fourth reason was that the student may just not have worked hard, and it is easier to put them into someone else's class than to coax them into learning. The bottom line, though, is that, for the times, the Binet and Simon tests were well intentioned and were properly seen as serving a positive function.

Binet's view of intelligence is very different from many current views. It is difficult to believe, at times, how far modern scholars in the field of intelligence have departed from Binet's views, despite their often having used tests that are a direct successor of his. One way in which they have departed is in the popular belief that a given level of intelligence is something you are born with and, thus, kind of stuck with, for better or worse. Binet did not believe intelligence is fixed. Rather, he planned later in his life to devise what he referred to as "mental orthopedics," or exercises to help young people increase their intelligence. He never got around to it – he died before he much got started, at least to our knowledge.

Why would Binet believe that intelligence is modifiable when so many of his successors did not believe the same? Quite simply, he must have seen improvements in children's intellectual skills. Binet was an academic but also a practitioner. He did not just collect numerical data. He observed children and how they functioned. But later scholars had an incentive not to believe in modifiability. That is because the study of intelligence during the early years of the twentieth century got swept up in racial and political ideology. As history has shown over and over again, those who wanted to believe in the inferiority of certain (socially defined) races or ethnicities found it convenient to believe not only that there were differences in scores on intelligence tests, but that these differences would persist forever more because the groups were born different and always would be different (Sternberg, Grigorenko, & Kidd, 2005). For example, if a politician wanted to exclude members of certain groups from foreign lands from immigrating to the United States, it was convenient to exclude them because they were alleged not to be smart enough – which is exactly what was alleged. Unfortunately, some politicians still do this, catcalling to prejudiced people in the hope of getting their votes when they come up for election or re-election.

Binet's test was followed by a competitor test, one proposed by psychologist David Wechsler in the United States (Wechsler, 1940, 1944). Wechsler defined intelligence as "the aggregate or global capacity of the individual to act purposefully, to think rationally and to deal effectively with the environment" (p. 444–445). Notice how in tune Wechsler's definition of intelligence is with Binet's. Wechsler too believed that intelligence is something that does not just happen when one takes a test, but rather is about adaptation to the environment in which one lives or may live.

Binet's definition of intelligence is as relevant today as it was in 1916 (or 1905, when it was first published in French). You want to be smart? You won't find your smarts by studying for or taking a lot of IQ tests or proxy tests – SATs, ACTs, GREs, or whatever. Instead, be careful and deliberative in your judgments – about people, about things, about events. Find direction in your life. Show initiative. Take responsibility for your thoughts, your actions, and your life. Make something of yourself. Adapt to the environment, or if you cannot, try to find a new environment that works better for you. You want to show people you are smart? Do not tell them about your standardized test scores or your admission to a high IQ society. Show them that you can make rational, sensible, and adaptive judgments. Binet understood intelligence much better than do the test purveyors of the 21st century! If you are a child, worry not just about what you can show on a test, but also about what you can do with the knowledge you have to make a difference in your home, school, and extracurricular environments.

Binet's contribution today may seem rather smaller than it did at the time. After all, intelligence tests in the Binet tradition have been around for more than a century. What was the big deal? The big deal was that Binet's predecessor, Galton, was on a totally different track. Binet recognized that.

2.1.2 Francis Galton: Intelligence as Energy and Psychophysical Sensitivity

Binet was not actually the first major psychological theorist to define intelligence. I put him first because, in terms of historical significance, he was unquestionably the most important. But preceding him was Sir Francis Galton, who viewed intelligence in a very different way. Binet not only had to come up with his own conception of intelligence, he also had to battle against the Galtonian conception, which at the time carried a lot of weight and is still influential in some circles today.

Galton wrote two major works concerning intelligence (Galton, 1869/1892/ 1962, 1883/1907/1973). Galton had a background very different from Binet's (see www.intelltheory.com/galton.shtml). He was a first cousin to Charles Darwin, so clearly grew up in an extremely eminent family. He explored Africa and was a Fellow of the Royal Geographic Society. He was an ardent eugenicist – indeed, he coined the term "eugenics." He was a statistical expert and contributed to the development of many of the statistical concepts used today in the study of intelligence. In his later life, he even became a knight of the British Empire.

Galton proposed two general qualities that, in his view, distinguished people who were more intelligent from those who were less intelligent. These two qualities, he believed, were essential if one wanted to be intelligent in one's life.

The first of the qualities was *energy*. We all see every day that some people are full of energy. Others seem to have very little energy. They are lethargic and have trouble getting themselves to do much of anything. They would rather sit around or do something that does not require them to work hard. Galton believed that this difference in energy was part of intelligence. So, Galton was actually the first major theorist to propose what today might be called a "motivational" theory of intelligence. Galton did not see intelligence as one thing and motivation to use it as another – a more common view today. Galton viewed them as part and parcel of the same thing. Those who sit around and do nothing with themselves were not just lazy, in Galton's view; they were less intelligent because they made so little of themselves. Binet was later to pick up on this aspect of Galton's definition when he talked about the importance of initiative. For example, some children are brimming with energy and enthusiasm to learn; others sit at their desks, just waiting for the school day to end.

The second of the qualities was *sensitivity*. It was here that Galton went wrong, I believe. When Galton talked about sensitivity, he was not talking about whether someone is easily disturbed or upset. Rather, he was talking about a particular type of *psychophysical* sensitivity – that is, sensitivity to physical stimuli. As a result, he believed that the keys to intelligence were sensitivities to pitch (Can you hear a very faint tone? Can you recognize which of two tones is higher in pitch?), odor (Can you distinguish between two different but very similar odors, or can you smell the odors at all?), visual cues (How faint a light can you see? Can you say which of two similar light sources is brighter?), and tactile cues (Can you detect a very light pin prick? Can you tell whether two pins pricked you at exactly the same point?). In his book on inquiries into human faculty and its development (Galton, 1883/1907/1973), he said: "The discriminative facility of idiots is curiously low; they hardly distinguish between heat and cold, and their sense of pain is so obtuse that some of the more idiotic seem hardly to know what it is. In their dull lives, such pain as can be excited in them may literally be accepted with welcome surprise" (1883, p. 28).

This statement is quite a mouthful. It tells you what Binet was up against in turn-of-the-20th-century France, and I would argue that it tells you what we all are up against still. Many of the sentiments he expressed then can still be found today. It is easy to see how, in a Galtonian world, children with any kind of physical or psychophysical handicap would be viewed as "stupid."

First, Galton viewed those with intellectual challenges as fundamentally different from you and me. We do not take pleasure in pain. We do not, for the most part, live dull lives – or, at least, dull in the sense to which Galton referred, where we look at pain as a relief from our dull lives. He viewed the intellectually challenged as "apart": as not part of mainstream society. This mindset continued long after Galton, with many of those who were challenged, institutionalized, or otherwise separated from normal existence. They were viewed as shameful or somehow as not "whole" people.

Second, Galton adopted an extremely disparaging attitude toward those who live with intellectual challenges. That attitude was very common in Galton's times and is, unfortunately, not uncommon today. There are organizations, such as the American Association on Intellectual and Developmental Disabilities, that seek to protect the rights and privileges of those with intellectual challenges, but they have their work cut out for them today as in the past. Unfortunately, the disparaging attitude Galton had toward those with intellectual challenges persisted for much of the history of the field, with esteemed scholars of the early 20th century, such as Henry Goddard, taking pride in taking pokes at those who are intellectually challenged. The field could have done better; for the most part, it did not. This precedent of disparaging people with differences persists among some to the present day, and is a loss to us all, as it separates us rather than brings us together. Children throughout history have been deprived of life opportunities because so much of society shared Galton's view that children with challenges were little more than a burden on society.

Third, Galton viewed intelligence as based largely on psychophysical processing. This view was shown later to be a huge mistake. Stephen Hawking was one of the greatest astrophysicists of all time and yet lived with severe psychophysical challenges because of his illness (a form of amyotrophic lateral sclerosis [ALS]). Helen Keller was universally acknowledged to be one of the most brilliant people of her time, and yet was deaf and mute. Ludwig von Beethoven, in his later life, would have failed any Galtonian test of pitch sensitivity or pitch discrimination, and yet was one of the great composers of all time – for some, *the* greatest. At the same time, there have been people with excellent physical skills – Aaron Hernandez of the New England Patriots comes to mind – who made a total mess of their lives through their poor judgment.

Fourth, in his book *Hereditary Genius* (Galton, 1869/1892/1962), Galton made clear that he believed intelligence to be largely inherited – passed down through families in a biological way that left little to influences other than the biology of one's parents. So, if one ended up being on the lower end of the intellectual continuum, there was not much anyone could do about it, or even should try to do about it. One was where one was on the intellectual continuum because of biologically deterministic forces over which one had no influence.

Galton's views on intelligence were brought to the United States by a scholar at Columbia University named James McKeen Cattell. Cattell went beyond Galton in developing tests that measured many of the psychophysical abilities that Galton had speculated were central to intelligence. For example, he developed a test of how tightly one could squeeze one's hand, of how quickly one could move one's arm from rest to a distance of 50 cm, of the distance between two points on the skin that was needed for one to feel pricks of a pin as occurring in different places, and so on.

Cattell's research had a bitter ending, at least for Cattell. One of his students, Clark Wissler, found Cattell's claims to be, in the ways that mattered, wrong (Wissler, 1901). In particular, scores on Cattell's tests neither correlated with each other, nor did they correlate with students' grades at Columbia University. This was a major blow to Cattell and his theorizing, because if psychophysical tasks truly measured intelligence, then one would think that they would correlate with each other and with measures of academic success.

2.2 Lessons from the Galton–Cattell Experience

We can learn a lot about intelligence from the Galton–Cattell experience. Here are four lessons.

First, the field of intelligence has a long history of sidelining people with intellectual challenges – treating them as "different" and disparaging them. It is a shameful history. But as author William Faulkner observed in his novel *Requiem for a Nun*, "The past is never dead. It's not even past" (Faulkner, 2012). Many people continue to emphasize the differences between themselves and those with intellectual challenges, and to disparage them. Those who do so should keep in mind that if we dig deeply enough, we all have intellectual and other challenges, no matter who we are. It is sad when we need to boost our self-esteem by disparaging others.

Second, intelligence is not to be found in trivial tasks, psychophysical or otherwise. A tendency that has been common in intelligence research over the years has been to try to find very simple origins of intelligence. For example, Arthur Jensen was one of a number of researchers who sought to understand intelligence by analyzing people's performance on choice reaction time tasks. A participant would see two or more lights, and then quickly push the designated button to indicate which had flashed. The participant's intelligence was supposed to be a function of how quickly they reacted to the light (i.e., reaction time) (Jensen, 1998). His evidence was the same as much of the evidence in this field. Choice reaction times showed a relatively modest but statistically significant (meaningful) correlation with scores on intelligence tests. The problem is that almost any cognitively based behavior shows a modest but statistically significant correlation with scores on intelligence tests. The evidence was weak. But scholars are just as susceptible to confirmation bias as everyone else. When they manage to see data as confirming what they want to believe, no matter how much of a stretch, they believe.

Third, scholars are like anyone else: they often are willing to follow trends to advance their careers, even when the trends are counterproductive and lead them away from the truth. Thomas Kuhn was among the first to recognize how little innovation there really is in science, as in other things (Kuhn, 2012). For the most part, scholars work within already established paradigms, no matter how good, bad, or ridiculous they are. They just follow what others have done before them, making small innovations. So, Galton had outsized influence on the field, setting up the field in a way from which it still has not fully recovered. Kuhn pointed out that paradigms are overthrown not all at once, but only slowly and often painfully as they prove increasingly incapable of answering the questions that really matter for a field.

Fourth, intelligence of course has a biological component, but in nothing like the way Galton believed. I will discuss this issue at greater length later in Section 4.2. But intelligence is not biologically deterministic and there is much one can do to improve, at least to some degree, one's intelligence – one's real intelligence as judgment and adaptation to the environment, not just as scores on a bunch of not very consequential intelligence tests.

My colleagues and I have suggested that most of science consists of what we have called "forward incrementations" – small steps forward from where the field has been at a given time (Sternberg, 1999c; Sternberg, Kaufman, & Pretz, 2002). Scholars, educators, and others like small steps forward because they are nonthreatening and do not cause anyone to risk their career. They lead to nice pats on the head. They basically serve as compliments to the scholars who came before. And so many have paid tribute to Galton by continuing with his disparaging attitudes and his separation of intellectual elites from others. Richard Herrnstein and Charles Murray's book, *The Bell Curve*, is a good example of this (Herrnstein & Murray, 1994). Instead of saying that some children achieved at less than desirable levels at least in part because they grew up in poor environments and went to poor schools, it claimed that children grew up in these poor environments largely because their parents were not very bright and could do no better than to land themselves and their children in these inferior environments. And more, they believed, like Galton, that the intelligence you are born with is largely the intelligence you are stuck with.

The field of intelligence research needed what my colleagues and I called a "redirection" – a change in direction away from disparagement, emphasis on the inferiority of intellectually challenged people, and emphasis on heredity. Binet provided that. And yet, despite Binet, the field went in a direction that probably would have made Galton much happier than Binet. What happened?

Binet and Galton offered initial accounts of intelligence but neither proposed what would be called a full-fledged theory of intelligence. Their successors did offer such theories. The theories sometimes have been used more to pigeonhole children than to provide them with optimal opportunities.

3 Psychometric Conceptions of Intelligence

While Binet and Wechsler were pushing for a broad conception of intelligence related to real-world functioning, another group of scholars was headed in a rather different direction. In particular, they were focusing on the nature of intelligence as exhibited not so much in the everyday world, but rather as exhibited on intelligence tests. For these scholars, intelligence was basically what the tests measured – no more, no less.

3.1 Defining Intelligence as What Intelligence Tests Measure

The field of intelligence, as we know it today, was built largely around the presupposition that intelligence is whatever intelligence tests measure (Boring, 1923). This presupposition was first made by the British psychologist Charles Spearman (1904) and is still accepted by many scholars in the field of intelligence and much of society today (see Sternberg, 2020).

Why is it a mistake to assume that intelligence test scores, and scores on proxies for intelligence tests such as the SAT or GRE or related standardized tests, can be equated with intelligence, as much of the field does, and many laypeople do today? Consider three reasons.

First, this equation automatically excludes anything else that might be relevant to intelligence. Creative thinking? Not on the tests. Common sense? Not on the tests. Wisdom? Not on the tests. Emotional intelligence? Not on the tests. Social intelligence? Not on the tests. Initiative actually to get something meaningful done? Not on the tests. By limiting the scope of what is called "intelligence," scholars who are devoted to intelligence tests have thrown everything else in a kind of "discard bin." Creative children may be iced about of educational and other opportunities because they do not think in the cookie-cutter mold rewarded by conventional tests of intelligence.

Second, when tests are validated – shown to be measuring what they are supposed to be measuring – they are often correlated with other tests. In other words, the validation procedure is set up, at least in part, automatically to look good, because the tests all measure roughly the same thing so they generally will look good. If anyone comes up with a test that does not measure the same thing but nevertheless measures skills relevant to everyday life adaptation, that test will not look so valid. The reason is that scores will be compared with scores on other conventional intelligence tests. But the new test will not correlate well with conventional intelligence tests because it goes beyond what those tests measure. In other words, the system is extremely conservative, favoring tests that keep doing what tests have done before.

Third, the system of definition is obviously circular. One would think such a basic point of logic would have been noticed, but it apparently eludes many scholars. How do you know what intelligence is? By what the tests measure. How do you know what the tests measure? By the definition of intelligence as what the tests measure. Once you enter the circle, you are in a situation analogous to that of someone who drives into a traffic circle determined never to leave it or perhaps even to notice that leaving it is an option: Intelligence is defined in terms of intelligence test scores; intelligence test scores are defined in terms of intelligence.

3.1.1 Charles Spearman: Two-factor Theory of Intelligence

Among academic researchers of intelligence, Charles Spearman (1927) is perhaps the most famous scientist ever. His most important work argued that intelligence comprises two kinds of factor: general intelligence, or g, and specified factors, or s. On this theory, there is a general ability that is measured by *all* tests of intelligence, regardless of the kinds of questions they ask. This general ability is what Spearman considered to be most important in understanding intelligence. Spearman's view is still widely held today (see Kaufman, Schneider, & Kaufman, 2020).

The idea is that if you have an intelligence test that has, say, some vocabulary items, some arithmetic items, some reasoning items (e.g., TALL : SHORT :: FAT :?), some spatial items measuring your skill in visualizing objects in space, and so forth, the general factor will permeate all of them. No matter what questions the tests ask, the general factor of intelligence will be involved in your answering them. When children grow smarter with age, it is largely because of increases in the effective functioning of their general factor of intelligence.

This emphasis raised an obvious question: What, exactly, is the general factor of intelligence? Just calling it a "general factor" is obviously nothing more than giving it a name. What is its psychological source? In 1927, Spearman did not know; he suggested it might be something he called "mental energy." It is not entirely clear what Spearman meant by "mental energy," but it seems to be some kind of ability to focus deeply and for an extended period of time on a problem that presents a mental challenge.

If you look at the general factor developmentally, you can understand Spearman's view of the development of intelligence. In his view, people are born with more or less of the general intelligence they will have throughout their lives, relative to other people their own age, but not relative to people of other ages. As children grow up, their level of *g* increases, but other children's levels of *g* also increase, so that people hold about the same rank order, relative to each other, throughout their lives.

The general factor (*g*) is derived from a statistical technique called "factor analysis" that Spearman invented, and it literally is a single factor, or source of individual differences, in this method. It is some kind of single, hypothetical construct. But is intelligence really a single thing?

3.1.2 Godfrey Thomson: Theory of Bonds

Godfrey Thomson, a Scottish psychologist, suggested that the general factor, *g*, is actually not a single thing; rather, it is an agglomeration of many things, or what he referred to as "bonds" (Thomson, 1916). On Thomson's view, attributing *g* to just a single psychological process was a mistake unjustified by the data Spearman obtained. Here is his logic.

Suppose that every test a child (or adult, for that matter) takes requires a certain grouping of skills. For example, all of them might require (a) paying attention, (b) understanding directions, (c) following those directions, and (d) providing an answer to each question. We already are up to four skills that answering every question requires. But because every single question requires each of these skills, they might all get glommed together in the statistical technique of factor analysis. That is because the statistical technique separates abilities on the basis of different tests requiring different abilities. So here, all of the abilities in the mind will be separate, but in the results of a factor analysis will appear to be a single ability.

Why does this matter? There are at least three reasons. First, statistical analyses are always open to interpretation – and, sometimes, radically different interpretations. The analyses may be presented as though the interpretation is unequivocal. It almost never is. Second, statistical analyses always make hidden assumptions that readers about the techniques, and often even users of the techniques, are unaware of. In this case, what appears to be one thing truly may be many things, even though the assumption Spearman and many others made was that one factor signified just one psychological process. Third, and most importantly, the difference between Spearman's and Thomson's interpretation of the results was major. In other words, differences of interpretation are not just matters of details. Sometimes, they are matters of fundamentally different ideas that lead to radically different conceptions, here of intelligence, depending on who is looking at the results, and how they are looking at them.

From a developmental point of view, Thomson's theory has implications that are quite different from Spearman's. It's not just one big thing that develops, such as mental energy. Rather, many different skills (bonds) are developing in tandem. To become smarter, children must learn a wide variety of skills and how to coordinate them. The skills may be related to each other, but they are nevertheless psychologically distinct.

3.1.3 Louis Thurstone: Primary Mental Abilities

Louis Thurstone, an American psychologist at the University of Chicago, believed that both Spearman and Thomson were wrong. Thurstone proposed what he called a theory of primary mental abilities (Thurstone, 1938). According to this theory, intelligence is neither one big thing (Spearman) nor a huge number of very small things (Thomson). Rather, it is an intermediate number of things – in particular, seven things:

1. Verbal comprehension (measured by tests such as vocabulary and reading comprehension)
2. Verbal fluency (measured by tests asking test-takers to generate as many words of a given kind as quickly as possible – for example, words beginning with the letter "m")
3. Number (measured by tests of arithmetic skills)
4. Spatial (measured by tests requiring visualization of what objects look like when they are rotated in space)
5. Memory (measured by tests requiring recall of what one has learned)
6. Inductive Reasoning (measured by tests requiring figuring out and applying rules, such as completing a series of numbers or letters)
7. Perceptual Speed (measured by tests requiring rapid perceptual processing, such as dotting i's and crossing t's)

Thurstone, like Spearman and Thomson before him, used factor analysis to support his theory. He just used it in a different way. He ended up with the seven factors described above. He and Spearman got into a rather heated argument over whose theory was right.

Thurstone's theory has a different set of implications for the development of intelligence. In Thurstone's theory, these seven abilities develop with age. If you want to work on your intelligence, with this theory you at least have something concrete you can do. With the theory of *g*, it is not clear what you can improve. With Thurstone's theory, it is much clearer. Grow your vocabulary; read more and pay more attention to what you read; improve your arithmetical skills; practice visualizing what objects would look like when rotated in space; devise mnemonics (tricks) to learn new things. All these skills can be taught in school. Thurstone's theory was the first to clearly suggest what it is you should do to improve your intelligence.

3.1.4 J. P. Guilford: The Structure of Intellect

J. P. Guilford believed, at various points in his career, that intelligence comprises 120, 150, or 180 distinct mental abilities. Guilford's theory has not stood up well against the test of time. His way of statistically analyzing intelligence data (Guilford, 1967, 1988) proved to be seriously flawed (Horn & Knapp, 1973). Guilford's theorized abilities may have been valid, but his claim that the abilities were independent was not valid.

Guilford believed that each ability comprised a content, a process, and a product. The abilities were identified by crossing these three elements. For example, cognition (process) of verbal (content) relations (product) would be one ability in the theory. It would be the ability most central to analogical reasoning – for, example seeing the relation between "tall" and "short" in the verbal analogy, "tall : short :: fat : thin."

Guilford was one of the first to introduce creative and practical elements of intelligence into his model. He referred to creative thinking, or at least an aspect of it, as divergent thinking. This is thinking that produces more than one response, with responses usually given more credit if they are creative (i.e., novel and useful). He referred to practical thinking, or at least an aspect of it, as behavioral (i.e., involving actions people take in their everyday lives). He was thus the broadest theorist of intelligence up to his time. But when his theory was discovered to be statistically questionable (Horn & Knapp, 1973), intelligence researchers pretty much "threw out the baby with the bath water." The creative and practical aspects of Guilford's theory were not to appear later, at least in recognizable form, in the bulk of subsequent psychometric theories of intelligence. These aspects are harder to measure, and, in the case of divergent thinking, required multiple answers, which is almost a disqualifier for inclusion of an item in many psychometric tests.

There was an additional feature relevant to the inclusion of creative and practical skills in Guilford's theory that is worth mentioning: Such skills almost certainly are developed through experience. Children develop these skills by observing others using them and then by utilizing the skills themselves. Early theorists such as Sir Francis Galton believed creativity to be heritable, but later theorists of creativity generally were more open to other interpretations of the data.

3.1.5 Raymond Cattell's Theory of Fluid and Crystallized Abilities

Raymond Cattell was nothing if not a colorful character. He created a religion, Beyondism, which he claimed was derived from science (Cattell, 1987). He also had some rather strong prejudices. He was supposed to receive a major award from the American Psychological Association, but the award was withheld pending investigation because Cattell was accused of being a racist (Hilt, 1997). Unfortunately, as noted earlier, many early intelligence theorists (not necessarily Cattell) were racists. Some today might still be. In any case, Cattell died before the presentation of the award could be adjudicated.

Yet however strange – bizarre, even – his personal views might have been, Cattell's theory of intelligence has been extremely influential. Cattell believed that general intelligence has two interrelated components: fluid intelligence (g-f) and crystallized intelligence (g-c). Fluid intelligence comprises the set of skills one uses to solve novel, challenging problems, such as what number, letter, or shape would come next in a series, or what number, letter, or shape does not fit with others in a set. Cattell believed that fluid intelligence develops with age and gives rise to the second kind of intelligence, crystallized intelligence, which is essentially your knowledge base. Crystallized intelligence is most often measured by tests of vocabulary or general information. For example, you might be asked what a synonym would be for "habile" (skillful) or the name of the predecessor organization to the United Nations (League of Nations).

Although I discuss cultural bias in more detail in Section 6, it is worth observing now that it is extremely difficult, if not impossible, to create a test of intelligence that is culturally "neutral." The vocabulary and general information one acquires depend very much on one's cultural background and one's socialization experiences. Why would anyone outside the United States know the name of the second president of the USA (John Adams), any more than anyone outside Australia would be expected to know the name of the second prime minister of Australia (Alfred Deakin)? This knowledge is culturally specific – as, indeed, is almost all other knowledge. It used to be thought that tests of fluid abilities – say, using abstract geometric forms – are more culturally fair. But they are not. It turns out that in some cultures children learn about abstract geometric shapes, but in other cultures they do not. And even the act of taking a test is cultural (Sternberg, 2004). Children from a collectivistic culture might expect to collaborate on an important task such as taking a test. In other words, as we shall see in more detail in Section 6, all intelligence tests draw on cultural experiences.

3.1.6 John B. Carroll: Three-stratum Theory

John B. Carroll has proven to be one of the most influential intelligence theorists. Toward the end of his career, and after he retired from his job in research at the Educational Testing Service, Carroll perused all the published factor analyses he could find that met his minimal criteria for being well constructed. Through this analysis of 461 factor-analytic data sets, Carroll constructed what he called a three-stratum theory of intelligence. At the bottom of the hierarchy were very specific factors and at the top was general intelligence (Carroll, 1993). What were most important to the theory were the abilities in the middle, namely: fluid intelligence, crystallized intelligence, decision speed, cognitive speediness, retrieval fluency, memory and learning, auditory perception, and visual perception. This model appears to fit well with data for four-year-old children (Bornstein & Putnick, 2019).

Carroll's theory has been expanded upon still further in what has come to be called CHC theory, with the initials referring to *C*attell, *H*orn (a student and collaborator of Cattell), and *C*arroll (McGrew, 2005). But this expansion basically builds on Carroll's theory.

3.2 What Can We Learn from Psychometric Theories?

The psychometric theories – those that derive from psychological measurement – almost certainly have been the most influential in intelligence theory, research, and assessment. Contemporary intelligence tests, such as the Stanford-Binet and the Wechsler, have been reorganized in their scoring so that they yield scores that correspond to elements of CHC theory or some other contemporary theory. What can we learn from these theories?

The first thing is that the theories are *all* based on the results of conventional intelligence tests, in the traditions of Binet and Wechsler. So, the theories are only as good as the tests. If the tests are lacking in their conceptualization – if they are too narrow – so are the theories. One can get out of a factor analysis only a transformation of the data one puts in.

The second thing we can learn is that academics are very good at splitting hairs. The theories are splitting hairs because they are all based on the same kinds of data. One can argue about whether the data mean this, that, or some other thing, but ultimately virtually none of the theorists went outside their comfort zone, namely using fairly conventional IQ tests to generate theories of intelligence. They are post hoc – after the fact – theories. The researchers gave tests, analyzed the data, and then constructed theories based on the ways the data looked to them. The theories differed because the theorists chose to see different stories being told by the data. Most of the data sets could have been looked at as supporting one theory or another, depending on the way the researcher chose to look at the data.

The third thing is that the researchers were mostly conventional in their choice of the criteria they used to validate their tests. They used other tests, which of course correlated because the tests all measure pretty much the same thing (what Spearman referred to as g, plus some other things, such as shrewdness in figuring out how to take tests and ability or willingness to follow directions). The researchers used school grades and school performance, which should correlate with IQ test scores because Binet originally created his tests to predict school performance and the tests did somewhat well at it. They should, as schools require test-taking and often use material related to that on IQ tests. And they also have used various longer-term measures of individual success, such as health outcomes, income, level of professional accomplishment, and so on. What they did not look at was how people actually solved IQ test problems, or at the biological bases of the cognitive processes people used. The next set of theories, considered in Section 4, has explored such matters.

4 Cognitive and Neurocognitive Conceptions of Intelligence

Cognitive and neurocognitive theories of intelligence seek to understand intelligence in terms of how people process information about the world and to understand the brain-based mechanisms underlying this information processing. Whereas a psychometric theory might describe *reasoning ability* as a factor of intelligence, a cognitive theory (also called an "information-processing theory") seeks to understand the basic information processes people use when they solve a reasoning problem. What do people do, in real time, to reach a solution to the problem? How does what they do develop over time, from the time they are young children to the time they are adults? What kinds of strategies work and what kinds do not? And how are these processes derived from the functioning of the brain and central nervous system? Cognitive and neurocognitive approaches once were viewed as distinct, but today are often combined because each subapproach relies on the other.

Cognitive theory developed largely as a reaction to psychometric theories. Cognitive theorists believed that psychometric theories are, more or less, labeling exercises. The idea of cognitive theories is to understand how people actually think when they think intelligently.

4.1 Cognitive Theories

4.1.1 Arthur Jensen: Speed of Neuronal Conduction

One of the simplest models of information processing as a basis for intelligence was proposed by Arthur Jensen, among others (Jensen, 1998). It was discussed briefly in Section 2. Jensen asked what intelligence might be in terms of the processing of the nervous system – in other words, his approach was both cognitive and neurocognitive. The theory he advanced is that intelligence is based on speed of neuronal conduction. According to this theory, smarter people have neurons (nerve cells) that process information more quickly. People whose neurons process information more quickly can not only process more information per time unit, they then are free to process other information that would get stuck in a bottleneck if information were processed more slowly. Jensen purported to measure speed of neuronal conduction indirectly by using a choice-reaction time task. A child who could process information more quickly would learn faster, and, ultimately, would know more. The participant would see a light, which would guide them to choose one or another button to press. The more quickly they could react to the light, on this view, the smarter they were. Although mental speed appears to be related to intelligence, it is not clear that this mental speed actually relates to speed of neuronal conduction. Also, it is not clear how much differences in speed of neuronal conduction, if they existed, would translate to everyday activities that require far longer periods of time than the small numbers of milliseconds per response involved in studies relating choice reaction time to neuronal conduction.

4.1.2 Earl Hunt: Speed of Retrieval of Information from Long-term Memory

An early information-processing account of intelligence was proposed by Earl Hunt (Hunt, Lunneborg, & Lewis, 1975). Hunt suggested that intelligence, or at least verbal intelligence, could be understood in terms of very simple information processes – that is, complex processing is actually based on fairly simple information processing. Hunt suggested that verbal intelligence derived from the speed with which a person could retrieve information from long-term memory. In other words, when you try to remember something, how quickly can you retrieve that information?

4.1.3 Robert J. Sternberg: Speed, Accuracy, and Strategy in Complex Information Processing

In my own early work, I proposed that views such as those of Arthur Jensen and Earl Hunt oversimplified intelligence. Instead, I proposed that to understand intelligence one needed to look at the more complex processes involved in intelligence, such as those that required the mental processes of setting up problem solving and then actually engaging in it. In solving real problems, people need to go beyond reaction times or retrieving information from long-term memory. They need to think in complex ways; they need to make inferences; they need to apply those inferences; they need to justify answers that may not be quite correct as either good enough, given the complexity of the problem, or else try to find a better answer.

In this theory, the mental processes and attitudes underlying intelligence are common across all times and places (cultures), even if what people need to do to execute them successfully differs from one time or place to another. The main processes are these:

• *Recognition of the existence of a problem.* To solve a real-world problem, people first need to recognize that the problem exists. In the COVID-19 pandemic, the stunning incompetence of many leaders in failing to recognize the existence of a problem has led in the United States to hundreds of thousands of unnecessary deaths. If social distancing had started even a mere week earlier, 36,000 lives might have been saved (Chappell, 2020). Unfortunately, the deaths are not limited to the United States. As of the day I am revising this text (September 29, 2020), more than a million people have died worldwide from COVID-19. Experts had been predicting for years that there would be a pandemic, likely caused by a virus of some kind (Henig, 2020). Problems can be solved only if people first recognize that they exist. This issue, of course, is not limited to pandemics. Many marriages fail because individuals do not recognize until too late that their marriage is going seriously downhill (Sternberg, 1998b). Children often undergo years of abuse because they do not recognize they are being abused and hence do not report the abuse – or because they are afraid to report it if they do recognize it. And many of the problems we have today as a result of climate change were also recognized long ago, as carbon levels in the atmosphere started to rise. Even Exxon, a major source of carbon pollution, recognized the growing problem more than 40 years ago (Hall, 2015). One could say that ignoring problems of carbon emissions helped companies such as Exxon, but, in the long run, if there are no humans on the Earth because of global climate change, there will be no Exxon (or similar corporations) either. So, we have companies that have people smart enough to recognize the existence of serious problems; yet, collectively, they have failed to acknowledge them, with disastrous results.

- *Definition of the problem.* It is one thing to recognize the existence of a problem; it is another to figure out exactly what the problem is. Definition of a problem refers precisely to the specification of what the problem is that one is facing. For example, someone may know that something is amiss in their marriage or in any intimate relationship, but not know exactly what it is, and so either does nothing or, possibly worse, solves the wrong problem. This definition of the problem is the greatest challenge facing scientists studying COVID-19 today. At this point, virtually all of them have recognized what the problem is – starting with the fact that people are dying prematurely in startling numbers. But why is this happening? What, exactly, is the problem? Why are older people more susceptible to COVID-19 than younger people? Why are obese people more susceptible? Why do some people show no symptoms and others die? Basically, scientists have figured out that COVID-19 is caused by a novel coronavirus, but they have not figured out what the scope or definition of the problem is. Why is the virus doing what it is doing? By the time you read this, perhaps these answers will have appeared. As I write, they have not.
- *Allocation of resources to the problem.* Almost all of us have too much to do. We need to allocate our time, energy, money, and other resources to invest more in solving some problems than others. Standardized tests measure such time allocation on a mini-scale because they require allocation of test time across the items of a test. But the stakes are generally small, and there is very little emotion associated with, say, one item versus another, whereas in everyday life, some problems may lead to great emotional investment and others to little or none at all. Moreover, in everyday life some problems seem far more important than others, whereas on tests, most of the time each problem counts equally toward the total score. In other words, no differential sets of rewards and punishments are associated with solving either some items or other items within the time allocated. COVID-19 required a great deal of investment. But had the investment been made before the problem mushroomed, that investment of resources would have been much more effective than it turned out to be when people waited until the last minute, or beyond, to solve it.

- *Representions of the problem.* When we need to solve a problem, we first have to find some way of representing it. For example, some people have defined the COVID-19 pandemic as a problem primarily of people sickening and dying. They are representing the problem in terms of the stakes for human lives. Other people have represented the problem primarily in the economics of jobs – how many jobs and how much income are lost. Still others have represented the problem in terms of the trade-off between the two, with differing weights for the cost in human lives versus lost jobs and income. How you represent the problem will have serious consequences for how you attempt to solve the problem and what solution you produce. For example, those who have represented the problem in terms of illnesses and deaths generally have advocated only slow reopenings of businesses and other institutions; those who have represented the problem primarily in terms of jobs and income lost generally have been more eager to see businesses reopen. Representation can lead one to solve a problem one way or another, depending on what the representation is.

- *Construction of a strategy to solve the problem.* Once a problem is represented, it needs to be solved. Or, if it cannot be solved as represented, it may need to be re-represented. In the case of COVID-19, a number of steps have been proposed and implemented, such as social distancing, minimizing contacts, wearing masks, closing businesses, setting aside hospital wards for COVID-19 patients, contact tracing, frequent and widespread testing for COVID-19, and so forth. The strategies highlight an essential feature of successful intelligence – that it is about realized potential, not potential in the abstract. There are lots of good ideas for tackling COVID-19; the problem is getting them to work and keeping people following them even after they are sick of them! The chosen strategy needs to be one that is good not only in theory, but one that will work in practice.

- *Monitoring the strategy while it is being implemented.* Most of us have heard the expression that "the devil is in the details." So it is with many of the strategies we construct in our lives. Masks are a great idea for reducing transmission of disease, but they are useless if people do not have them or do not use them, or use them only occasionally, or use them as necklaces rather than over their faces. Social distancing is great – so long as people actually do it. Minimizing contacts is great, so long as people do not make more and more exceptions to the rule. Any strategy, when executed, needs to be monitored. One reason why so many of our plans in life fail is not necessarily that they are inadequate when they are conceived, but rather that circumstances change or may have been nonobvious at first, and therefore our plans need to be changed to accommodate reality.

- *Evaluation of the strategy.* After one is done solving a problem – perhaps well after one has finished solving it– one has to evaluate whether the strategy worked. Sometimes the strategy seemed to be successful while it was being executed, but afterward seems less successful. For example, social distancing seemed to be working until many people got sick of it. Masks have worked and might have worked better had not unscrupulous politicians decided that their election prospects were more important than preserving lives. All strategies need to be evaluated after execution, because, no matter how good they are, circumstances change, and hence so may the effectiveness of the strategies.

As noted, each of these strategic steps involves both an attitude and a skill. The attitude pertains to whether one wishes to execute the step. The skill pertains to how well one executes the step. Both are important. Without both, the step fails somewhere along the line. Anyone in the time of COVID-19 could wear a mask to prevent COVID-19, but many would get sick, and some would die, because, although they had the basic skill, they lacked the attitude.

I tested the componential theory using a method I have called componential analysis (Sternberg, 1977a, 1977b, 1983). I would present participants with problems such as the following:

1. *Analogies.* What is the solution to the analogy: *lighten : darken :: raise :?*
2. *Series completions.* What is the next number in the series: *2, 5, 9, 14,?*
3. *Classifications.* Which word does not belong with the others: *giraffe, whale, robin, dog?*
4. *Linear syllogisms.* John is taller than Bill. Sam is shorter than Bill. Who is tallest?
5. *Categorical syllogisms.* All fliks are dworps. All dworps are klegs. Are all klegs dworps?
6. *Verbal comprehension.* The *blen* arose on the horizon. What does *blen* mean?

I measured response times to these problems and also computed error rates. The problems were systematically varied to make them differentially difficult. I considered:

- What mental processes did the participant use in solving each problem?
- How long did each process take in real time?
- How error-prone was the process?
- How did the participant represent the information mentally?
- Into what strategy did the participant combine the processes?

Why is all this information important, anyway? Why should anyone care?

Componential analysis is important because traditional IQ tests and their proxies give a distorted view of intelligence. For example, consider an analogy that might appear on a verbal test: *mitigate : assuage ::? : exacerbate*. The test is supposed to be a measure of verbal reasoning. But is it? Mostly, it measures vocabulary. If you do not know what the words mean, you cannot solve the problem.

Similarly, consider the math problems on an IQ-test proxy, such as the SAT or ACT. Where does one learn the mathematics one needs to solve the problems? The answer is obvious: in school. So, what about the difference between a student whose parents pay many tens of thousands of dollars to send them to an elite private school and a student whose parents who rent a shabby apartment and send them to a school where math is barely taught? And then, the math may be taught by teachers who spend much of their time dealing with a lack of resources and various cultural issues, such as students who speak many different languages, in their classrooms. Is this, in any sense, fair? Do all children have the same opportunities to learn what "assuage" means, or what any low-frequency English word means?

The problem is that abilities and achievements are not distinct – they are on a continuum. As Binet recognized, achievements are developed abilities. I have even suggested that abilities are a form of expertise that is developed through home and school (Sternberg, 1998a, 1999b). In other words, when we measure abilities such as intelligence, we are measuring, at the very least, indirectly, achievement. There is no pure measure of abilities. The goal of componential analysis was to separate out the reasoning components from the knowledge operating on those components. In this way, any test based on componential analysis would be more nearly fair to test-takers and would separate out their school-based achievement.

4.1.4 Alan Baddeley, Meredyth Daneman, Randall Engle, Patrick Kyllonen, Andrew Conway, and Others: Working Memory

In recent times, many investigators have focused on the role of working memory in intelligence (Ellingsen & Engle, 2020). Working memory refers to the information you need at a given time to solve the problem at hand. In other words, it is the activated part of long-term memory that you need to solve a problem. What are you thinking about as you solve the problem? In the initial version of the theory, the idea was simply that people who had more capacious working memories – working memories that could store more information – would be more effective problem solvers and hence more intelligent in problem solving. Many theorists still hold to this view.

Randall Engle and his colleagues suggested a more complex variant on this theory (Engle & Kane, 2004). They suggested that working memory is important, but that it always works in tandem with so-called fluid intelligence (which was discussed in Section 3.1.5). They believe that the role of working memory is to store information, but the role of fluid intelligence is actually to drive out of our minds information that is not relevant to the solution of the problem at hand. We almost always have more information in a real problem than we need to solve the problem. We need a way to forget, or at least, to put out of our minds, the information that will never be relevant, or that once was relevant but that no longer is, to our problem solving. So, according to this theory, working memory and fluid intelligence work together: the former storing and processing the information, and the latter getting rid of the information we never needed or no longer need. In this way, we are able to proceed efficaciously through the solution of a problem, from start to finish.

The strictly cognitive theories were a big step forward from the psychometric theories in that they specified in more detail how information is processed, rather than just naming abilities. But they did not specify biological mechanisms. A different theory has done so.

4.2 A Biological Theory: P-FIT (Parieto-frontal Integration Theory)

Rex Jung and Richard Haier have proposed a brain-based model of intelligence that integrates many of the findings of biologically oriented studies of the brain (Jung & Haier, 2007). Previously, many theorists thought that intelligence was primarily located in the frontal lobes (Haier, 2020). This model is different in suggesting that intelligence is distributed across the parietal and frontal lobes. Intelligence exists in the integration of functioning across the two lobes.

Work on brain correlates of intelligence has been done by Haier and his colleagues. In one set of studies, Haier and colleagues tested male participants on their ability to solve Raven Advanced Progressive Matrices, an iconic test of fluid intelligence (Haier et al., 1992). The participants were injected with a dye that would enter their brains and show which areas were active while the participants solved the problems. A control group of participants did an attentional task to control for having an activity, but one that presumably would not require higher mental functioning.

Several cortical areas were assessed for the differences in activation between the experimental and control groups. The results were surprisingly clear cut. There were correlations between scores on the Raven and levels of cortical activation. However, the correlations were negative, meaning that the higher performers showed *less* cortical activation. These results led to what has been called the *brain-efficiency hypothesis* – that higher performers show less acti-vation because, for them, the problems are easier. They simply do not have to work as hard to solve them (Haier et al., 1988).

In a later study, Haier and colleagues examined girls while they played a computer game called *Tetris*. Basically, the results, using a different experi-mental technique, supported the brain-efficiency hypothesis. Girls who per-formed better on *Tetris* generally showed less brain activation than the girls who were not as strong on the task (Haier, Karama, Leyba, & Jung, 2009).

Obviously, such studies do not address the question of *why* the problems were easier for the participants who performed more efficiently. What made them more efficient? This question should remind us that correlation is not tanta-mount to causation. We may find that the brain becomes more or less active in one person versus another. The deeper question is what it is that causes this to happen.

Biological approaches to the study of the brain are extremely useful, in that clearly our performance depends on the activity of the brain. What perhaps is needed most of all at this point is some further integration between biological theories, such as Haier's, and contextual theories (discussed later), that attempt to provide some understanding of what is intelligent for whom in what particu-lar environmental context. What parts of the brain are called upon as the context changes, and what is adaptive to environmental changes? More importantly, how do cognition and the biology of the brain fit into the world at large? Systems theories attempt to answer these questions.

Both cognitive and biological approaches help us understand the internal workings of intelligence. What they do not offer is a comprehensive account of how intelligence interacts with the environment. Systems conceptions do that.

5 Systems Conceptions of Intelligence

Systems conceptions of intelligence and its development deal with intelligence as systems of interaction between the individual and the environment rather than as a fixed set of factors, mental processes, or parts of the brain. Two major theories have been proposed to date: the theory of multiple intelligences, and the theory of successful intelligence.

5.1 Howard Gardner's Theory of Multiple Intelligences

Not all theories of intelligence have been based exclusively on psychometric data. Howard Gardner (1983, 2011) proposed a different kind of theory, which he referred to as a theory of multiple intelligences (MI theory).

Gardner claimed that the reason why investigators had not successfully targeted what intelligence actually is is because it is not one thing; rather, it is multiple things. There is no one intelligence; rather, there are eight distinct and relatively independent intelligences. These are not like eight factors precisely because, according to MI theory, they are independent systems rather than merely abilities subordinate to general intelligence. Thus, in Gardner's theory, the intelligences are not hierarchical – arrayed under general intelligence – but rather each is an independent system of functioning with its own activated modules in the brain and its own symbol system by which it is represented. Each child has a distinct system of mental functioning for each intelligence.

According to Gardner, the eight intelligences are:

1. *Linguistic intelligence.* This is the intelligence that is used to read, write, listen, and speak. Its symbol system is words. It is one of the eight intelligences that is measured, although not fully adequately, by many intelligence tests, in that most of them contain at least some verbal content. An individual high in linguistic intelligence might be adept at tasks such as debating, writing poetry or novels, writing newspaper or other articles for the media, giving speeches that are eloquent and well-organized, reading various kinds of material, understanding lectures on challenging topics, and the like. Children's linguistic skills develop naturally as they learn to read, write, speak, and listen. Schools are attuned to increase children's levels of linguistic intelligence. Parents also develop children's linguistic intelligence in their conversations with their children and in encouraging them to read and to listen to lectures or other presentations with serious verbal content.

2. *Logical-mathematical intelligence.* Logical-mathematical intelligence is involved in doing arithmetic problems, solving algebraic equations, solving geometry and trigonometry problems, computing change, balancing a checkbook, computing mark-ups on items for sale or computing savings on items that are on sale, solving logical puzzles, and the like. The symbol system is numerical or logical symbols. Schools emphasize the development of logical-mathematical intelligence, although generally not quite to the same extent as they emphasize the development of linguistic intelligence. Some teachers in the lower grades were not as well trained in mathematics and so are not as adept at teaching the skills involved in logical-mathematical intelligence as they might be at teaching linguistic skills. Many mathematical problems are presented as word problems, so may require a mix of logical-mathematical and linguistic intelligence. Traditionally, mathematicians, accountants, actuaries, statisticians, engineers, and economists have been high in logical-mathematical intelligence.

3. *Spatial intelligence.* Spatial intelligence is involved in imagining objects rotating in space; in finding one's way in a new environment; in imagining what a disassembled model of something, such as a model airplane or car, would look like if put together; in accurately reading a map; in visualizing how the various parts of a house are interconnected with each other; and so on. Spatial intelligence is developed through practice. Indeed, a study of cab drivers in London, who have to negotiate a particularly complex and unsystematic layout of roads in a very large, sprawling city, found that the volume of the hippocampus, a part of the brain involved in learning and visualizing, was correlated with the amount of time drivers had spent driving taxicabs (Maguire et al., 2000). In other words, merely by practicing the use of one's spatial skills in a systematic way, the brain changed to accommodate one's need to use the skills more effectively and, presumably, more efficiently. Experience can change the brain. Some of the jobs that require high levels of spatial intelligence are architect, civil engineer, graphic designer, builder, airplane pilot, and taxi or hired driver who does not make exclusive use of a GPS system.

4. *Bodily-kinesthetic intelligence.* Bodily-kinesthetic intelligence is involved in playing baseball or basketball or football, in gymnastics, in dance, in balancing oneself while walking on a thin elevated platform, in exercising, in running, and the like. Although some people obviously have better physiques than others for particular bodily-kinesthetic endeavors, children develop bodily-kinesthetic skills by careful, systematic training and by deliberate practice. Not everyone will be a Michael Jordan, the star basketball player, or a Nadia Comaneci, a child gymnast awarded a perfect score (10) at age 14 in the 1976 Olympics. But children can develop competence by building up the sets of skills various sports or other endeavors require, coordinating them and learning to deploy them strategically as needed. Jobs that require a high level of bodily-kinesthetic intelligence are professional athlete or gymnast, dancer, explorer, gym instructor or coach, acrobat, and mountain climber.

5. *Naturalist intelligence.* Naturalist intelligence is involved in identifying and classifying patterns in nature. For example, one would use this intelligence to identify the names of trees by the patterns and colors of their leaves; to recognize poisonous plants, such as poison ivy; to recognize different species of animals in a forest; to acquire a feeling for when there will be a major degradation of the weather; and so on. Some of the jobs that require a high level of naturalist intelligence are nature-study counselor, forester, entomologist, game warden, farmer, botanist, and horticulturalist.

6. *Musical intelligence.* Musical intelligence is involved in singing, playing a musical instrument, composing music, appreciating music that one listens to, and dancing, among other things. Its main symbol system is musical notes, but there are other symbol systems as well, such as those used in choreography. People are probably born with quite different levels of musical intelligence. But musical intelligence needs to be developed; it does not just manifest itself in the absence of systematic instruction or years of practice (Ericsson & Poole, 2017). Occupations that require a high level of musical intelligence are composer, orchestra or band player, chamber music player, instrumental soloist, member of a professional choir, vocal soloist, and orchestra or band conductor.

7. *Interpersonal intelligence.* Interpersonal intelligence comprises the set of skills we use to relate to other people. It is similar or identical to what others call "social intelligence." Interpersonal intelligence is developed through our interactions with other people – our family, our friends, our teachers, our coworkers. Many jobs require substantial interpersonal intelligence to be done effectively. Jobs that require a high level of interpersonal intelligence are psychotherapist, psychiatrist, actor, social worker, manager, admissions officer, clergy person, and tour guide.

8. *Intrapersonal intelligence.* Intrapersonal intelligence involves the skills needed for self-understanding. This kind of intelligence is developed through increasing self-reflection and metacognition – understanding of one's own cognitive processes. Most of the jobs that require high intrapersonal intelligence are ones that also require a high level of interpersonal intelligence. But intrapersonal intelligence might be additionally important for living in a monastery or a convent, or in any kind of group setting where one's nature becomes particularly obvious to others and affects how the others live.

Although Gardner has grouped the intelligences into eight categories, the eight categories, statistically, appear not to be independent, as Gardner proposed. Rather, they appear, at least in some cases, to be correlated with each other (Visser, Ashton, & Vernon, 2006). It also is not clear that the intelligences really are unified modules in the mind. For example, some people are good readers but not particularly good writers. A mathematician may be very good at abstract higher mathematics, but not at arithmetic computation, whereas an accountant may be good at computation but not at abstract higher mathematics. Similarly, someone may be a good musical performer but not be able to write good musical compositions, and composers are not necessarily excellent instrumentalists or singers, for that matter. Or someone may be a great basketball player but turn out to be only a middling baseball player, at least at the professional level (as was Michael Jordan).

The other issue that has come up with Gardner's theory is how far one wants to go in defining a set of skills as an intelligence. If we look at intelligence as adaptation to the environment, as Binet and Wechsler originally suggested, it is straightforward to see, at least in many cultures, how linguistic or logical-mathematical intelligence would be essential to adaptation; but perhaps, today, it is harder to see how bodily-kinesthetic or musical intelligence would be essential to adaptation to the environment. Helen Keller and Stephen Hawking (mentioned in Section 2.1.2) adapted very well and both became very eminent, yet they each had severe bodily-kinesthetic limitations. Many people have the proverbial "tin ear" for music, but perhaps no one would know it in the course of normal everyday life if they were not musicians.

Some might argue that at least some of Gardner's intelligences more closely resemble talents than skills. That said, Gardner had a set of criteria he used to define an intelligence, and the ones he offered in his theory were the ones that met his criteria. Not everyone, however, would agree with his criteria – which were created somewhat subjectively – or with his evaluation that all the chosen intelligences fully met those criteria. For example, it is not clear how much psychometric support (one of his criteria) there is for the existence of bodily-kinesthetic, naturalist, or intrapersonal intelligences.

Because the scientific support for Gardner's theory is so mixed, some psychologists have taken it less seriously than I believe it deserves to be taken. In particular, Gardner was among those, following Guilford, who recognized how very limited psychometric conceptions of intelligence are. He expanded the range of abilities that could be considered under the rubric of intelligence. He may have gone too far, but some might argue that a capacious view of intelligence, which allows more children (as well as adults) to show what they are capable of, is more justifiable than a narrow, constricted one.

5.2 Sternberg's Theory of Successful Intelligence

I have proposed a theory of successful intelligence that, like Gardner's theory, is broader than standard psychometric theories, but that is based more strictly on empirical scientific data collected to test the theory (Sternberg, 1997, 2003).

Augmented Theory of Successful Intelligence. The augmented theory of successful intelligence holds that intelligence is to be found in a person's skill in creating a set of goals for their life, making plans that fit their goals, and then trying to reach those goals, in the process transforming the goals and plans as necessary to fit changing life circumstances. Almost all of us, at one time or another, believe we are on one road in life, only to find later that we need to change our plans. As is sometimes said (only partly in jest): God laughs at people's plans.

This view of intelligence means that intelligence involves the same processes for everyone, but how these processes are executed differs widely from one person to another. What would be good life planning, say, for a would-be musician or developing musician might be very different from what would be good life planning for a would-be physician or a developing physician. Actions that might make sense in one cultural milieu might make no sense at all in anther cultural milieu.

To be a good life planner, one needs to figure out what one's strengths and weaknesses are, and to capitalize on the strengths and compensate for the weaknesses. In other words, one has to figure out what one's contribution is and how one can go about making this contribution. People may all have somewhat different contributions to make, and so they may be successfully intelligent in different ways. There is no one "right" path in the way that there might be a "right" path in trying to solve an IQ test problem. Life does not much resemble an IQ test.

Four skills and attitudes are especially important for achieving success in life, at least, for many people. *Skills* refer to how well someone can do something, given the life experiences that someone brings to a task or situation. *Attitudes* refer to one's desires to do that thing – is one interested in doing it? The theory of successful intelligence is unlike other theories of intelligence, perhaps, in that it is action oriented. It is not just about what one can do, but also about what one wants to do – and what one ultimately does do. It is about intelligence in action. There are any number of people who, say, could find a way to help needy others in particular situations. But without the attitude of wanting to help, knowing how to help makes little or no difference. And beyond that, successful intelligence is about translating these skills and attitudes into action.

The four skills and attitudes that are highlighted in the theory of successful intelligence are creative, analytical, practical, and wisdom-based. Creative skills and attitudes are used to generate ideas that are both novel and useful in some way. Analytical skills and attitudes are used to decide whether those ideas are good ones – are they sensible, logical, meaningful, achievable? Practical skills and attitudes are used to implement one's ideas and to persuade others that the ideas are worth pursuing. And wisdom-based skills and attitudes are used to ensure that the ideas help to achieve some kind of common good – that they help not only oneself and one's family, or people like oneself and one's family, but also those tribal affiliations and interests that may be different from one's own. To be successfully intelligent, then, one must generate creative ideas, analyze their quality, put them into practice and convince others of their value, and, ultimately, seek out a common good one can realize through those ideas.

The theory of successful intelligence implies that analytical, creative, and practical skills are somewhat distinct when applied to everyday life. All of them draw on the same processes, but their instantiations in everyday life are different.

My colleagues and I conducted a series of studies to assess the validity of the theory of successful intelligence. In one set of studies, we administered to students at the high school and college levels tests of analytical, creative, and wisdom-based skills (Sternberg, 2010; Sternberg, Bonney, Gabora, & Merrifield, 2012; Sternberg & the Rainbow Project Collaborators, 2006). The Rainbow Project tested high school and college students from around the country who had diverse levels of abilities. The Kaleidoscope Project was used for actual admissions to Arts, Sciences, and Engineering at Tufts University over a period of a number of years. A third project was called Panorama. The results were revealing. In the Rainbow Project, our measures roughly doubled prediction of first-year college grade-point average. At the same time, they reduced substantially the ethnic group differences that are found on traditional tests of intelligence and their proxies. The Kaleidoscope Project also increased prediction and almost entirely eliminated ethnic group differences. The increase in prediction applied to academic performance and to quality of extracurricular performance. In both this project and the Panorama Project, students were admitted to the respective universities who otherwise would never have been admitted. These were students who later showed their ability to succeed in the college environment, but who would not have been admitted using standard criteria. They were students who were creative, practical, and/or wise – attributes not measured by conventional intelligence tests and their proxies.

It is possible also to teach based on the augmented theory of successful intelligence – to develop students' creative, analytical, practical, and wisdom-based skills (Sternberg, 1998d, 2013; Sternberg & Grigorenko, 2007; Sternberg, Jarvin, & Grigorenko, 2009). In one study, high school students came to Yale University for a summer program in introductory psychology (Sternberg, Grigorenko, Ferrari, & Clinkenbeard, 1999). The participants were chosen to be in one of four skills groups: high especially in analytical skills, high especially in creative skills, high especially in practical skills, high in all three (analytical, creative, and practical), or not especially high in any of these skills. Then the students were randomly assigned to one of four instructional conditions – standard instruction emphasizing memory, instruction emphasizing analytical thinking, instruction emphasizing creative thinking, or instruction emphasizing practical thinking. At the end of the course, we assessed all the students' achievement through tests that measured understanding of the material in terms of memory learning, but also analytical, creative, and practical learning. In a nutshell, students performed best when they were taught in a way that, at least some of the time, matched their pattern of skills. (Note that this discussion pertains to *skills* in learning and thinking, not to *styles* in learning and thinking, which are another matter.) In other words, if you want students to learn in an optimal way, challenge them in ways that enable them to capitalize on their strengths and to correct or compensate for their weaknesses.

In other work, we showed that analytical or academic intelligence is relatively independent of practical intelligence. They are largely different things (Hedlund, 2020; Sternberg, Wagner, Williams, & Horvath, 1995; Sternberg et al., 2000; Sternberg & Hedlund, 2002). Someone can be high in practical intelligence or common sense, and yet not very high in IQ – or vice versa. Or they can be high in both, or low in both. The one tells you little about the other. Indeed, the world seems to be full of people whose academic intelligence becomes useless as soon as they step outside the doors of a school or a university; other people have a great deal of common sense but do not have the levels of academic skills of some of their peers.

The way we discovered the relation of practical to academic intelligence is that we created job-related tasks for a number of different occupations, such as salesperson, manager, and teacher. We asked people to answer questions about how to solve problems on these jobs. All the test items required tacit or informal knowledge – what you need to know to succeed in a job that is not explicitly taught and that often is not even verbalized. We found that tests of practical intelligence showed only minimal correlations with tests of academic or analytical intelligence. In other words, being practical is different from being school smart. But being practical does not always mean being adaptive, in a larger sense.

Theory of Adaptive Intelligence. In the most recent development of the theory, which I have referred to as *adaptive intelligence,* I have argued that our preoccupation with intelligence tests has resulted in our grossly misconceiving what intelligence is about (Sternberg, 2019c, in press). As Binet and Wechsler made clear, and as has been made clear in multiple early definitions of intelligence, intelligence is, above all, the ability to adapt to the environment. Other attributes may be desirable for intelligence, or possibly even essential, but adaptation to the environment trumps them all. This is because, in a Darwinian sense, sustained existence of a species, in general, and of a particular gene pool, in particular, comes down to adapting to the environment. If organisms of a certain gene pool (species, family, or whatever) do not adapt, they go extinct. For humans, adaptation is biological, in the larger sense, but is mediated by the sociocultural context in which people live. What is considered adaptive may vary from one culture to another. But what is adaptive, regardless of the particular behavior, results in an individual's living long enough to reproduce. If a species were to create a situation in which they could not reproduce, the species would go extinct, as most species, over time, have gone (Simberloff, N.D.).

Here is an example of a problem my collaborators and I use to measure adaptive intelligence:

Water pollution

You live in Collier County, Florida, in the United States of America. The water bodies nearby are polluted with red tide organism – harmful algae blooms (*Karenia brevis*) – due to dumping of chemicals (nitrogen- and phosphorus-based) and nutrients. The sources of red tide are commercial agriculture and industries near the county. This condition makes the water unfit for healthy living conditions. Many respiratory irritations, liver conditions, and skin problems have been observed due to airborne toxins from the bloom. In 2016, the Government of Florida announced a state of emergency due to loss of aquatic life and public health risk. In 2017 and 2018, the area suffered through an unusual, persistent, toxic red tide for a long period. Now, in October 2019, there is an abrupt increase in red tide, *Karenia brevis* 1,000,000 (cells/liter), which has caused an emergency red alert.

1. What could you do personally about the problem?
2. What is wrong with what is being done (or not done) about it now?
3. What would you recommend those in authority do about it?
4. What are the obstacles to doing what needs to be done about it?"

This problem deals with water pollution. Other problems we use deal with air pollution, global climate change, COVID-19, bacterial resistance to antibiotics, weapons of mass destruction, increasing income disparities, poverty, and related topics.

So, suppose a species somehow considered itself to be quite intelligent. Why would it consider itself intelligent? Perhaps because of high IQ scores – higher than any other species (of course, on the tests that that species conveniently created to measure intelligence). If another species created the tests, perhaps that species instead would look more intelligent. But suppose that species, which considered itself to be intelligent, acted in such ways as to hasten its own demise. For example, maybe it contributed grossly to global climate change, making the world gradually uninhabitable for members of that species. Or maybe, in the face of a disease pandemic, some of its leaders acted in ways that systematically hastened illnesses and deaths, either by ignoring the disease or by actually staging events that inevitably would lead to its spread. And suppose some people mindlessly followed those leaders. Or perhaps individuals acted in ways that worsened air and water pollution, resulting in illnesses and deaths that otherwise would have been easily preventable. In such cases, which would be a better indication of intelligence in any meaningful biological sense: preservation of a gene pool (whatever it may be), or attaining a high IQ score on tests loaded with problems that have little or nothing to do with adaptation to the environment and for which high scores might lead (and actually have been leading) to species extinction?

If, at some point in the distant (or not so distant) future, visitors from another planet came to visit Earth, and found that *Homo sapiens* had acted in ways so as to extinguish their own species, would those visitors consider *Homo sapiens* to be intelligent, or perhaps to be the stupidest species that ever inhabited the Earth? Dinosaurs lasted on Earth for 180 million years (Locke, 2008). Humans, as we know them today (*Homo sapiens*), have been around for roughly 200,000 years, and human civilization as we know it has been around for roughly 6,000 years. That means that human civilization, so far, has lasted 0.000033 as long as the dinosaurs, or 0.0033 percent. Does anyone seriously believe that, the way humans are going today, we will reach even 1 percent of the longevity of the dinosaurs, or perhaps even 0.1 percent or 0.01 percent? If humans are so intelligent, why are they doing such a truly awful job both of adapting to the environment and of shaping it in ways that make their future survival even plausible? Why do they purposefully engage in destruction of the very environment that they need to survive?

When I was young, I learned that lemmings were a unique species in that they committed mass suicide by jumping into water. It turns out that this was only an urban myth. But it is not an urban myth that human-induced climate change, pollution, and introduction of toxins into the environment are killing people (Sternberg, 2016, 2019a). From the standpoint of the theory of adaptive intelligence, intelligence is not only individual but also collective. Intelligence tests measure only the individual part of intelligence, and a very limited individual part at that. Somehow, we need tests that assess collective intelligence – people's responsibility toward each other and toward their descendants and those of others (Malone & Woolley, 2020). And we need to teach children in school not only to be individually intelligent – intelligent in ways that benefit the individual but that may be indifferent or even harmful to the collective (Sternberg, 2016, 2017, 2019b, 2019c). If we do not, then any notion of intelligence may hasten the rise of individuals who use their so-called "intelli-gence" to exploit each other, but at the expense of helping to achieve a common good. Ultimately, any notion of intelligence that is species-preserving must take into account how people can help to achieve a common good that will benefit not just them, but others as well. This collective good includes people of different cultures, with different conceptions of what it means to be smart.

To summarize, systems conceptions offer a view of the interaction of the person with the environment. Cultural conceptions provide more details about how people organize and interpret their environments.

6 Cultural Conceptions of Intelligence

Intelligence manifests itself quite differently in different places. Consider first accounts of intelligence in terms of adaptation to the environment. Then consider what people mean by intelligence.

6.1 Intelligence as Adaptation to the Environment in Diverse Cultures

In rural Kenya, the skills needed to adapt – to be intelligent – are quite different from the skills we are used to in the industrialized West (Sternberg et al., 2001). One of the most important skills there will at first likely sound very different from ones that matter to you, the reader. This skill is to know what to do when you contract an illness – specifically, a parasitic one. Examples of a few such diseases, which are common in rural Kenya, are malaria, trichuriasis, and schistosomiasis. The first is transmitted by mosquito bites; the latter two are transmitted by worms that enter the body.

Here is an example of a problem that measures the skills relevant to adapta-tion for these children:

"A small child in your family has homa. She has a sore throat, headache, and fever. She has been sick for three days. Which of the following five Yadh nyaluo (Luo herbal medicines) can treat homa?
  i. Chamama. Take the leaf and fito (sniff medicine up the nose to sneeze out illness).*
  ii. Kaladali. Take the leaves, drink, and fito.*
  iii. Obuo. Take the leaves and fito.*
  iv. Ogaka. Take the roots, pound, and drink.
  v. Ahundo. Take the leaves and fito."

The correct answers are asterisked. Chances are that you did not know the answers. That's ok. There is no reason you should know the answers. But for

Kenyan children, there is no particular reason they should know the answers to many problems that appear on Western intelligence tests. For them, the problem regarding natural parasitic medicines is relevant; to you, a problem such as the following, which might appear on a Western IQ test, is more relevant:

"What does the word *advocate* mean?
  i. doctor
 ii. proponent*
iii. opponent
 iv. judge"

The issue takes on a new level of complexity when one compares scores on a test of academic intelligence (IQ) with scores on our tests of intelligence as intelligence applies to the rural Kenyan context. We found a *negative* correlation, which is supposed to be virtually impossible – or, at least, *is* impossible if one believes very strictly in general-intelligence theory, as discussed in Section 3. Why would children who performed better on the rural Kenyan intelligence test perform worse on the conventional intelligence test, and vice versa? I believe there is a fairly straightforward explanation.

In much of Western industrialized culture, higher levels of education, which are associated with higher standardized test scores, are viewed as desirable. The higher the scores the better, in terms of passing through all the funnels society sets up for one to go from one level of education to the next, and from a less prestigious level of education to a more prestigious one. But imagine instead a system in which more education is viewed as the loser track. In this system, in rural Kenya, the students start off in school. The village tradesmen keep an eye on them. When they see a child whom they view as promising, they take the child on as an apprentice. Those children who do not attract the eye of any of the tradesmen stay in school. They are the ones in whom the society has little interest. So, ironically, the less interested the society is, the more education the children get, and hence the higher their academic test scores.

Although Western society is not identical, there are aspects of it that resemble the rural Kenyan situation. In particular, PhDs are not the highest-paid professionals. Many times, those with masters' degrees or even bachelors' degrees may out-earn PhDs.

The whole idea of measuring intelligence in terms of treating illnesses may seem quaint. But is it? As of the autumn of 2020, the United States has by far the worst record of COVID-19 cases in the world (www.theguardian.com/world/ 2020/sep/30/coronavirus-world-map-which-countries-have-the-most-covid-cases-and-deaths). We in the USA are seeing rising cases while most of Western Europe and many other industrialized countries are seeing falling numbers of cases. A political candidate recently held a campaign rally in a state with rising numbers of cases, and most attendees did not wear masks (Moreno, 2020). It is likely that a number of them will get sick and some will die. So, who is smarter: the typical rural Kenyan child without a formal education who knows how to deal with surging illnesses in their environment, or the Western educated adult who chooses a path that may lead to serious illness or death? Some adults have chosen an odd, species-defying course of action – "Live free – and die" – but for what (Times Editorial Board, 2020)? Intelligence is not just IQ. It is also keeping us and others alive by doing what the Kenyan kids do – preventing, recognizing, and treating diseases as they arise. In the USA, it may be a matter of political ideology, but how did spreading a deadly virus become a matter of political ideology? Is that adaptively intelligent or existentially stupid?

The problem of COVID-19 may be under control by the time you read this book. But here's the issue: It is a problem with devastating effects in the short-term. So the world sees the problem all at once. With most problems in the world, the effects are spread out over the long-term. So, the world will not see them until, as with COVID-19, it is much too late, and with consequences even worse than for the pandemic. Indeed, as I write today (August 22, 2020), two wildfires are raging in California that are the second and third worst in the state's history. Can the world afford to wait for these problems to become so serious that they are irreversible?

Now imagine children living in Yup'ik (Native American) villages in very rural Alaska. The children have many skills to learn in order to survive. For one, they will need to learn to navigate a dogsled in an environment where many of the spatial cues we are used to – road signs, intersecting streets, highly differentiated landscape, and the like – are absent. For another, they will have to learn to hunt, gather, and ice-fish. They need to know how to store goods for the winter, so that they will have enough and so that the goods will not spoil. Goods can be bought, but the only access to many of the villages is by airplane, if there is an airplane that stops there; and in the winter, the airplanes often do not fly. Even if they do fly, because the goods are flown in, they are very expensive in an environment where money is in short supply. And if intelligence is tantamount to adaptation to the environ-ment, then learning how to do all these things is, for these children, the development of their intelligence. In fact, we found that the Yup'ik children outscore children in urban areas of Alaska (well, as urban as they get!) in tests of adaptive skills for the Yup'ik environment, whereas the urban children outscore the Yup'ik children in more conventional tests of intelligence (Grigorenko et al., 2004).

Which children are "smarter": the rural Yup'ik children or the urban (and probably European American white) children? If one took the conventional intelligence tests to be ultimate measures of intelligence, then clearly the European American children would be assessed as smarter. These latter children have learned more of the skills that Western-style schools teach and expect children to learn. If you were to put the Yup'ik children in the schools of the urban children, they probably would lag quite a bit behind the European American children who grew up in the more urbanized environment. If you conducted a "validity" study to look at, say, prediction of grades in school, the IQ test would be shown to be valid, at least to a certain degree. It measured many (although certainly not all) of the skills necessary for academic success in Westernized schooling and the Yup'ik children were found to be lacking. End of story, right? But wait!

Now suppose you took the urban European American children and put them in the Yup'ik environment. Their adaptation will now be matter of their hunting, fishing, gathering, and related skills, such as navigating the frozen tundra with few visible landmarks. Here, the urban children might not look so smart anymore. They seem not to be able to do anything that matters – hunt, fish, or gather, for starters. They cannot find remote villages. Without a great deal of scaffolding from adults, they will look stupid. Left on their own, they will not survive for long.

Here is a problem used to test Alaskan participants:

"When Eddie runs to collect the ptarmigan that he's just shot, he notices that its front pouch (balloon) is full of ptarmigan food. This is a sign that:
- there's a storm on the way.*
- winter is almost over.
- it's hard to find food this season.
- it hasn't snowed in a long time."

Did you know the answer (starred)? Most of our Yup'ik children did. They are intelligently adapted to their own environment, just as you may be intelligently adapted to yours. But their environment, in all likelihood, is quite different from yours! The point is that what is adaptive depends on the environment in which you are socialized and in which you live. If you lived among the Yup'ik, you would need to be able to adapt to their environment, not yours. Your skills would probably ill prepare you, just as their skills ill prepare them for your environment.

In a parallel way, differences in the nature and manifestations of intelligence are closely linked to social class. For example, studies of street children in Brazil have revealed that the children often possess admirable arithmetical skills. For example, they can quickly compute change, discounts, or markups. But when confronted in the classroom, in abstracted academic contexts, with problems measuring the same skills which they can exercise with facility in the street, the children generally cannot do the problems (Ceci & Roazzi, 1994; Nuñes, 1994). This issue is not limited to street children in Brazil or elsewhere. In one study, 14-year-old boys performed at a low level on a task when the task was presented to the boys in terms of baking cupcakes. But the same boys performed well when the task was framed instead in terms of charging batteries (Ceci & Bronfenbrenner, 1985). A different investigator found that housewives in Berkeley, California who were able to do computations comparing prices of products in a supermarket setting often were unable to do the same computations on isomorphic (structurally identical) problems presented in classroom settings with hypothetical content (Lave, 1988). In a related study, Brazilian maids had no difficulty in performing tasks requiring proportional reasoning when the maids were hypothetically purchasing food. But they had great difficulty with the same task when hypothetically purchasing medicinal herbs (Schliemann & Magalhües, 1990).

These differences between the street children, or the housewives, and typical upper-middle-class children are highly consequential, although the testing industry and its enablers have ignored findings which are inconvenient for them. They are not alone, of course. Inconvenient findings are often ignored in science until a paradigm simply fails because it was always glaringly inadequate in the first place, as noted earlier in this Element (see Section 2).

The implication of such findings is that the existing tests are not only biased, but extremely biased against children of lower socioeconomic status. So why, then, does this statistical bias not show up in validity analyses that correlate intelligence test scores against external criteria of success? The reason is mindnumbingly simple: The criteria against which the tests are validated have the same bias as the tests themselves. When scholars validate an intelligence test or proxy against tests or other measures of achievement, both the intelligence tests and the measures of achievement, such as achievement-test scores or school grades, are typically based on academic problems presented in the context of schooling. The bias that exists in the predictor exists equally in the criterion. So, the test looks "fair." But it is fair only in the limited context of the school in which the test is administered. The test may be grossly biased for many criteria that would be measured outside school settings. Sometimes, more distal criteria are used, but how one performs on those criteria also depends in large part on the kind of education to which one has been exposed.

To be clear, the argument above is not to deny the existence of a so-called "general intelligence." General intelligence, as it is called, has been shown to be relevant to performance in a wide variety of tests and life endeavors. Rather, it is to argue that general intelligence is not enough. There is more to intelligence, defined as broad adaptation to the environment, than just what tests of general intelligence measure.

6.2 Changes in the Nature of Intelligence over Time

Sometimes, the nature of intelligence changes not only as a function of place but also of time. Patricia Greenfield has shown that the skills needed for success in pre-industrialized societies are quite different from those needed for success in industrialized societies (Greenfield, 2020). For example, pre-industrialized societies tend to be more collectivistic. Skills involved in working together tend to be very important and if people do not have them, they cannot intelligently adapt to the societies in which they live.

A dramatic immediate change in intelligence as adaptation took place in response to the downfall of the Soviet Union and its replacement by the Russian Federation (Grigorenko & Sternberg, 2001). In the Soviet Union, intelligence was conceived of much as it is in Western countries today, except that it likely was considered smart to keep one's mouth shut regarding one's complaints about the state. Otherwise, the secret police might well engineer a one-way ticket to Siberia, or worse. But after the fall of the Soviet Union, many jobs that had been important – jobs in government, for example – no longer existed. The skills that had been important for those jobs were no longer salable. Academic credentials also started to matter little. What mattered more was one's entrepreneurial skills in making money *despite* the changing political and economic system, not *within* it (Grigorenko, Ruzgis, & Sternberg, 1997). So people who, before the fall of the Soviet Union, would have been viewed as the losers who worked outside the system, were suddenly the smart ones. The ones who had been smart or brilliant, including university professors, were lucky if they were paid for their services.

The same, of course, is true for our ability to cope with COVID-19. As mentioned earlier, no other developed country is doing as badly as the United States in combating COVID-19 (Goldberg, 2020). One could, of course, blame President Donald Trump's seeming indifference to the pandemic, with his not wearing a mask, staging an indoor rally in Tulsa, Oklahoma, that likely infected large numbers of people, and saying, falsely, that the United States has beaten back the pandemic (Wise, 2020). No one has to listen to him, or to anyone else. But many do. The skills people need to stay alive – so as to be able to reproduce and rear children – have changed. People apparently have not. They risk their own and others' lives so they can continue to do what they have done in the past (Bardon, 2019).

The most stunning examples of changes in the nature of intelligence are in the skills that matter for adaptation today versus just a few decades ago. When I was a child, being a bad speller was considered to be a serious adaptive disadvantage. Schools were very concerned, with good reason, about poor spellers. Spelling still matters today, but much less so because spellcheckers in our computer software correct most of our spelling mistakes (and sometimes introduce new ones). Arithmetic computation used to matter a lot, but today calculators and computers do much of the computation that once had to be done on paper or in one's head. Spelling and arithmetic computation are now much less important than they used to be. The Wechsler intelligence test contains a test of general information, but today one does not need general knowledge in quite the same way one once did – much of it can be (and is) gotten through a quick search of the Internet. And the general information that matters changes, too. A test of general information would become outdated very quickly today. History does not change so fast – but the problems of contemporary significance, the general information that matters to our daily lives, changes very quickly. COVID-19 did not even exist – certainly not in humans, to our knowledge – before the end of 2019 (which is why it is referred to as a "novel" coronavirus). And there will be other pandemics People hope each one will be the last; it never is – at least, not so far!

Today, people in many places, especially the United States, are showing their failure to change their adaptive intellectual skills in response to the environment. They are more worried about how tests like the SAT are being delayed during the period of COVID-19. If you think about it, this is ironic. Many people are risking their lives daily by gathering intimately in areas with poor air circulation, in large groups, without wearing masks – and they think they need a test like the SAT to tell them how intelligent they are. Their mindless behavior says much more about their adaptive intelligence than the SAT ever will.

A good example of how adaptive intellectual skills change over time is in changing attitudes toward survivalists, or "preppers": people who are preparing for some kind of major catastrophe. For a long time, survivalists were looked at by many as an oddball sideshow, much as are people who are members of extremist religious cults. These are people who, in some cases, are devoting their lives and their financial and other resources to preparing for the worst. I, like so many others, always viewed them as a bit past the outer fringe of rationality. But today, the tilt of articles in the media has changed, with articles exhorting that "We Should All Be Preppers" (Garrett, 2020). Many of these individuals were (and are) ready for the pandemic and do not have to worry about their food or other supplies running out if things keep getting worse, as is the case in many parts of the world and of the United States. Adaptive challenges change over time. High IQ, high SAT scores, or prestigious college degrees mean little if, because one was unprepared for changes in adaptive requirements, one is dead.

Dystopian novels like *The Road* have, for many years, shown how the skills needed to survive and thrive in a Hobbesian dystopia – a *Lord-of-the-Flies* environment – are different from those needed to manage in the world that we are used to (McCarthy, 2007). These are skills such as being aware of people approaching even though one cannot see them yet and can hardly hear them; recognizing whether people one does meet are likely to be friends or (possibly deadly) foes; treating oneself for injuries, some of them fairly serious; finding food in environments where food is extremely scarce; surviving in harsh weather; and so forth. In the earlier history of humanity, before humans took the form we have today, people lived in something close to such an environment much of the time. They were not always at the top of the so-called "food chain." They had to worry about other species, and about other developing hominids (Smithsonian Institution, 2018). The COVID-19 pandemic may remind us of how little has changed both since then and since the earlier plagues that afflicted humanity and that many of us thought were events of the past.

At the same time that some skills become less important over time, other skills become more important. What are some skills that have become more important with time?

One skill that has become more important with time is *knowing how to retrieve information from the Internet, or anyplace else.* The amount of information available on the Internet is staggering. It is distributed in many different places. Any online search is likely to reveal staggering amounts of information. The Google search engine does not guarantee that the most important information is in the first few lines of a Google search, or even on the first page of results. How can you find the relevant information you need? My colleague Janet Davidson and I have called this *selective encoding* (Sternberg & Davidson, 1999). Here is a problem with intelligence tests and their proxies, though: For each problem, they give you the information you need to solve the problems. They do not measure how well you can retrieve possibly obscure information because they present you with the necessary information.

A second skill that has become increasingly important is information evaluation. In times past, newspaper and magazine editors evaluated information for us. If information was published, at least in a fairly reputable source, we could trust it. When I was young, there were three major television networks carrying nightly news: CBS (with Walter Cronkite), NBC (with Chet Huntley and David Brinkley), and ABC (with Howard K. Smith). Although the news anchors all had different styles, the news they carried was basically the same. Today, different media carry very different news. One would hardly recognize the same world events by listening to Fox News, with its strong right-wing slant, versus NPR, with its more middle-of-the-road slant, versus MNBC, with its strong left-leaning slant. Facts seem to matter little to some of the news outlets – at least, those representing the extremes. Some, such as One America News, can be expected to support President Donald Trump, no matter what he says or does; others, such as The Daily Beast, can be expected to oppose President Trump, also pretty much without regard to what he says or does. It is up to the consumer of media to find the truth that editors used to find for that consumer. One needs to be intelligent today to separate fact from fiction. One also has to believe that it matters to be able to do so, which brings us to folk theories of intelligence.

6.3 Folk Theories of Intelligence

Folk theories of intelligence, also called *implicit theories*, are people's conceptions of what intelligence is. We have seen how intelligence can be different things in different places and at different times. Similarly, what people consider to be intelligence can differ with time and place. The person who is considered smart in one time and place may be considered not so smart, or even stupid, in another time and place.

Before saying something about research findings regarding implicit theories, I need to say why they are important to understanding intelligence. Some people might say that folk theories do not matter much, because they represent only what people think intelligence is, not what it actually is. There are three arguments against this point of view.

First, the line between implicit and explicit theories of intelligence is not all that clear. We would like to think experts know a lot about intelligence and laypeople know little, but is that the case? Some experts have been pushing an antiquated account of intelligence for more than a hundred years. Experts often have trouble letting go of old ideas (Frensch & Sternberg, 1989). Maybe the problem has not been with laypeople's ideas, but rather with expert ideas?

Second, laypeople in diverse places often know best what the adaptive requirements of their own environmental contexts are. After all, they live it every day. Experts often sit in their armchairs and dream up theories they believe apply universally, or at least widely, without ever having visited or having a clue about many of the places and times for which they are positing their theories as relevant.

Third, the vast majority of judgments of intelligence are based on implicit, not explicit, theories of intelligence. We generally do not use test scores to judge other people's intelligence. Rather, we use job interviews, job performance, first dates, phone calls, and the like to judge people's intelligence. Our judgments of others are overwhelmingly based on how those others fit into our implicit theories of intelligence, not on their scores on some test of hypothetical reasoning and related skills.

What do studies of folk theories of intelligence show? In Africa, conceptions of the nature of intelligence center largely on the cognitive and other skills that help people to maintain and even to facilitate stable, harmonious, and mutually beneficial relations between groups (Ruzgis & Grigorenko, 1994). Relations within a group are equally important and, at times, even more important, as when groups experience internal discord that disrupts their functioning. As an example, adult members of the Chewa tribe in Zambia emphasize in their folk theory of intelligence the importance of social responsibilities, cooperativeness, and obedience as appropriate to the situation. Children who are intelligent are expected to be respectful of and obedient toward adults, including but not limited to parents and teachers (Serpell, 1996, 2002). In Zimbabwe, a word for intelligence is *ngware*, which actually refers to being prudent and cautious, especially in interpersonal relationships. Among members of the Baoule tribe, service to the family and to the community are considered important to intelligence, as are both politeness toward and respect for elders (Dasen, 1984). Parents of many Kenyan children further place emphasis on responsible participation in family and broader social life as keys to intelligent behavior (Super & Harkness, 1982, 1986, 1993). In a study of rural Kenyan conceptions of intelligence, my colleagues and I unearthed four distinct but interrelated terms underlying folk theories of intelligence: *rieko* (referring to knowledge and skills), *luoro* (referring to respect), *winjo* (referring to comprehension of how to handle real-life problems), and *paro* (referring to initiative in conquering new problems).

What I have found to be especially interesting about the rural Kenyan conception of intelligence is how close it is to the conception of the augmented theory of successful intelligence described in the preceding section. *Rieko* is close to the academic or analytical intelligence in the theory. *Luoro* is close to wisdom – respecting those whose knowledge and skills deserve respect. *Winjo* is close to practical intelligence. And *paro*, initiative in conquering new problems, is closest to creativity. Obviously, the matches are not perfect. But I cannot help wondering whether rural Kenyans might know something that industrialized Western experts do not know. Even in the United States, a culture that prizes standardized tests, my colleagues and I found that social competence and practical problem were an important part of folk theories of intelligence (Sternberg, Conway, Ketron, & Bernstein, 1981).

As you can see, emphasis on the social and general interpersonal aspects of intelligence is not limited to African cultures. Folk theories of intelligence in many cultures in Asia also emphasize the social, interpersonal aspect of intelligence more than does the conventional industrialized Western or IQ-based notion (Azuma & Kashiwagi, 1987; Lutz, 1985; Poole, 1985).

Of course, no country or culture has one unified folk theory of intelligence. For example, there is no one overall US or North American or South American folk theory of intelligence. One study found that different ethnic groups in San Jose, California, had different folk theories of intelligence (Okagaki & Sternberg, 1983). In particular, parents of Latinx schoolchildren often emphasized the importance of social competence and related skills in their folk theories of intelligence. In contrast, parents of Asian American children generally stressed the importance of cognitive skills, like those of learning, memory, and reasoning. Parents of European American (white) children also emphasized the importance of cognitive skills. The children's teachers, who were mostly from the dominant European American culture, generally stressed cognitive – rather than social – competence and interpersonal skills. The key finding was that the rank order of the various groups' performance in school could be perfectly predicted by the extent to which the parents of each group shared the teachers' folk theories of intelligence. Put another way, teachers generally rewarded most children who were socialized to be intelligent in a way that corresponded to the teachers' own folk theory.

This last finding bears more elaboration. We tend to think of children as "intelligent" to the extent that they perform well on tasks that society sets out for them. But what society? The society of the people in power. Children live not only in the world of the power structure – what has sometimes been called their *macrosystem* – but also in the world of their own social groups close to home – what has been called their *microsystem* (Bronfenbrenner, 2009). For a middle- or upper-middle-class child, the folk theory of intelligence in the microsystem may be essentially identical to the folk theory in the macrosystem. But for the child who comes from a culturally different background, those folk theories may be quite different, with the result that the child appears very bright in the context of the family and the immediately surrounding environmental context, but does not seem so bright in the context of the power structure of the larger society.

Perhaps the great difference in cultural conceptions of intelligence is in the extent to which they emphasize individualism versus collectivism (Markus & Conner, 2014). Traditional notions of intelligence, including psychometric and information-processing conceptions as well as Gardner's systems conception, have been very oriented toward the abilities and achievements of the individual.

The notion of adaptive intelligence, as introduced earlier, is much more oriented toward collective outcomes. Perhaps we have reached the point in the history of civilization when we need to recognize that we are all metaphorically in one big boat. The response to COVID-19 has highlighted that particularly well. Some of those whose primary concern was their individuality and their individual "freedom" to act however they wish (e.g., not wearing face masks) have ended up potentially sickening and possibly killing not only themselves, but also others. If that is smart, regardless of IQ, what is stupid? Cultural views of intelligence require us to think of intelligence as, at least in part, collective and cultural. If we do not do that, the pandemic will be only the first in a series of collective disasters that will hinder our ability to create a livable world for ourselves and for future generations. We need to think not only about ourselves, but also about our children, and our children's children. Developmental conceptions of intelligence, discussed in the next section, focus especially on children.

7 Developmental Conceptions of Intelligence

Developmental conceptions of intelligence seek an understanding of intelligence through an understanding of how intelligence changes in nature and in levels throughout the life span, from birth to death.

7.1 Quantitative Changes in Intelligence

Quantitative changes in development are those changes that are continuous. The concept of mental age illustrates this idea.

7.1.1 Mental Age: The Good, the Bad, and the Ugly

Alfred Binet, whose research was discussed in Section 2, believed that development holds the key to levels of intelligence. His test measured the same kinds of judgmental abilities from toddlerhood to old age, but the tests got harder as people got older. In the Stanford-Binet, the US American adaptation of Binet's work, a version of the test begins at age 2. A key concept introduced by Binet is that of *mental age*. One's mental age is the age of an individual whose normal mental functioning would encompass solving problems one can solve. If a child is 8 years old, meaning a *chronological age* of 8, and the mental age of the child is 8, then the child is functioning at the age one would expect for a child of age 8.

William Stern expanded on Binet's work by introducing the concept of intelligence quotient (IQ), which I have discussed throughout this Element without explicitly defining it. IQ is the ratio of mental age to chronological age, times 100:

$$IQ = \frac{MA}{CA} \times 100$$

IQ was computed as quotient through early editions of the Stanford-Binet and through many other intelligence tests, but is rarely computed in this way in current times. The reason is that the concept of mental age proved to be problematical.

First, mental ages, at least as measured by conventional tests, stop increasing in the latter teenage years, somewhere between ages 16 and 19. After those ages, people's scores stop increasing in a regular manner that is closely associated with chronological age. Second, as people grow older, their mental functioning often starts to decline. Declines start at different ages for different kinds of abilities and for different people, but at some point, if someone lives long enough, they are likely to start to decline. More importantly, abilities progress (and regress) at different rates for different people. Third, the concept of mental age suggests a smooth, linear increase in intelligence with age, an assumption that has not been borne out by data.

Today, IQs are computed by using percentile equivalents. IQs occur along a normal distribution, with most people near the center of the distribution (IQ of 100) and fewer and fewer people as IQs become more extreme. For example, an IQ of 100 places you in the top 50 percent of the IQ distribution. An IQ of 115 places you in the top 16 percent of the distribution. An IQ of 130 puts you in the top 2 percent of the distribution. And an IQ of 145 puts you way into the top 1 percent. The same would apply for scores below 100. For example, an IQ of 85 would place you in the bottom 16 percent of the distribution, and so forth.

Test publishers convert raw scores (number of items answered correctly) into percentile equivalents, and then in turn convert the percentiles into IQs. The IQ is no longer truly a "quotient." Rather, it is just a conversion from one scale (raw score) to another score (percentile) to yet another score (so-called IQ).

This concept of IQ, a term that was once based on a quotient, but no longer is, is tricky. But it is even trickier than it appears to be. This is because we now realize that an IQ of 100, or of anything, is not, as once was thought, a stable concept.

7.1.2 The Flynn Effect

James Flynn discovered in the 1980s that over the course of the 20th century, the number of items one needed to answer correctly to attain a particular IQ changed. In other words, the score that constituted, say, an average IQ, was not the same in 1900 as it was later in the century. In particular, IQ rose about 3 points per decade of the 20th century all over the world (Flynn, 1987, 2016). These IQ increases have not continued universally in the 21st century (Flynn, 2012). In some countries, IQs have continued rising; in others, they have remained steady; and in still others, they have started to fall.

The first obvious question to ask is, how, if average IQs have been changing over time, the average IQ could still be 100? If the average IQ was 100 in 1900, and IQs rose 30 points in 100 years (3 points per decade x 10 decades), in the year 2000 why wasn't the average IQ 130 instead of 100? The reason is that test publishers adjusted IQ scores to ensure that 100 stayed as the average. In other words, a raw score that would have brought you a 100 IQ in 1900 would have brought you an IQ of only about 70 in 2000! In 2000, you needed more answers correct to attain a given level of IQ. This means that, over secular time, IQs are not stable. They change, and who knows how much they have changed over periods of longer than a century? IQs develop not only over a person's lifespan, but also over time in the society surrounding the person. Some of the decline in IQ that once was thought to be due to a person's aging may just have been due to changing test norms (raw score–IQ equivalencies).

The second obvious question to ask is why IQs change over secular time. The short answer is that no one knows for sure. There probably is a confluence of factors, such as more and better education, better nutrition, better parenting, and changes in the demands of society. Flynn believes that the changes in IQ mostly reflect this last factor. Society expects more of us intellectually at some times than at others. With increases in technology (e.g., cell phones, computers, and other complicated devices that become part of our everyday life), people need to be cognitively more advanced to succeed in their environment. Those who are not cognitively more advanced are left further and further behind (which probably is exactly what is happening as economic inequality increases, not just in the United States, but in many countries around the world).

IQ, which has been promoted as this wonderfully stable concept, turns out not to be so stable, and, as I have argued in this Element, not so wonderful either. It is relatively stable, for most people, from childhood – at least from about age 8 – through most of adulthood (Deary, Whalley, & Starr, 2009; Deary, Whiteman, Starr, Whalley, & Fox, 2004). That is, although people's cognitive abilities change, their rank orders of IQ relative to other people remain relatively stable, unless they are subject to unusual cognitive interventions or they suffer acute cognitive decline, such as that associated with dementia. In the extreme latter years of life, as dementia becomes more common, all bets are off. There are just too many factors related to physical health that can affect IQ. But IQ is not all of intelligence. Not all of intelligence changes at the same rate as people grow older.

In particular, fluid abilities (discussed in Section 3) involved in dealing with novel and often abstract problems decline more rapidly, on average, than do crystallized abilities (also discussed in Section 3), which are associated with the acquisition, maintenance, and utilization of one's knowledge base (Hertzog, 2020a, 2020b). In general, fluid abilities peak somewhere between the ages of 30 and 40 and then begin a period of decline. Crystallized abilities can peak as late as the 60s, and then may begin to decline, although health conditions can greatly affect their course, as they can for fluid abilities. This developmental picture would be gloomier were it not for the facts that, first, there are wide individual differences in people's curves of growth and decline, and second, those who remain mentally active also tend to maintain higher levels of both fluid and crystallized abilities. People who have cognitively more demanding jobs also tend to fare better, probably because they have to remain mentally active in those jobs (Marquie et al., 2010; Schooler & Kaplan, 2009). Mental exercise probably helps maintain cognitive functioning, although the evidence is not unequivocal (Salthouse, 2006).

One would expect aging to be associated with changes in mental functioning, as the data show. Some theorists have even proposed that intelligence itself changes. There is mixed evidence for the so-called differentiation hypothesis – that abilities change in how differentiated they are at different ages. If abilities became more differentiated, it would mean that they split off – what starts off as one ability may become two or even three. It now appears that whatever differentiation occurs, it probably occurs in adulthood. Abilities also appear to be more differentiated in people of higher as opposed to lower cognitive abilities (Tucker-Drob, 2009).

Regrettably, perhaps, abilities show different patterns of development as a function of socioeconomic status. The abilities associated with IQ tend to be higher in those of higher socioeconomic status than in those of lower socioeconomic status. The shape of the growth curves also differs, with children of lower socioeconomic status tending to show decline in IQ with age (Von Stumm & Plomin, 2015). Because intelligence is largely socialized (Sternberg & Suben, 1986), it is not surprising that children growing up with parents who are less educated, who have had fewer opportunities in life, and who are from cultures that do not emphasize IQ-based skills might show different patterns of intellectual development from those children with more advantages. There is considerable research to suggest that the challenges these children encounter growing up (as described in Section 6) may have resulted in the children's developing abilities that their more advantaged counterparts may not have developed (Ellis et al., 2020). Nevertheless, a society that leaves many children behind cannot view itself as doing a commendable job of preparing those children for later life.

An alternative hypothesis to that presented above is that being of lower socioeconomic status is a result, not a cause, of lower cognitive abilities (Herrnstein & Murray, 1994; Murray, 2020). On this view, people of lower socioeconomic status are of this status because that is what their cognitive abilities allow them to reach. To the extent that the data show there are some genetic differences in intelligence, this hypothesis might seem reasonable (Knopik, Neiderhiser, DeFries, & Plomin, 2016; Plomin, DeFries, Knopik, & Neiderhiser, 2013). However, the genetic explanation seems to assume that genetic and environmental factors act largely independently. Evidence from epigenetics suggests that this is not the case (Hughes, 2014). Environmental factors affect how genes express themselves. Give children a bad environment and any genetic disadvantages they have, no matter how small, are likely to be amplified. And, as we saw in Section 6, having a view of intelligence as based only on IQ is to accept a narrow definition of the construct. The tests measure skills in which children of the middle- and especially upper-middle classes of technologically sophisticated societies are more likely to excel.

7.2 Qualitative Changes in Intelligence

Not all researchers of intelligence have taken a quantitative approach to intelligence and its development. Jean Piaget, a Swiss psychologist, took a qualitative approach.

7.2.1 Piaget's Genetic-Epistemological Model of Intellectual Development

Piaget suggested that cognitive development occurs through a process he referred to as *equilibration*, which is the balancing of a child's cognitive structures with the situations presented by the child's environment (Piaget, 1972). When children interact with the world, they inevitably find themselves in situations that do not fit their preconceived idea about the way the world is or should be. For example, the child may think that all pets are dogs. Piaget referred to this mismatch between the state of the world and the child's preconceived notions about the world as constituting a state of disequilibrium. He suggested that disequilibrium is good because it serve as an impetus for cognitive development. Piaget suggested that two cognitive processes can be applied to confront disequilibrium. Both processes instigate changes in children's cognitive *schemas*, or cognitive frameworks for organizing information about the environment.

The first process is *assimilation*, through which the child tries to incorporate new information into their already existing schemas. For example, if a child has a schema for dogs, and then sees a new kind of dog they have not seen before – say, a cocker spaniel – the child can assimilate the cocker spaniel as a kind of dog.

The second process is *accommodation*, by which the child creates a new schema to organize information that does not fit into preexisting schemas. For example, suppose the child sees a Siamese cat, which they previously thought was a dog but now realize is not a dog. They realize they need a new category and they figure out that the animal is an example of a cat. They then may create a new category for cats.

Piaget did not see repetitions of assimilation and accommodation as leading to continuous intellectual development. Rather, he believed that cognitive development occurs in discrete states, each building on, but qualitatively distinct from, the preceding one. The stages are always entered in a fixed, unidirectional order.

The *sensorimotor stage* occurs between birth and roughly age 2. In this stage, sensory and motor functions predominate. Intelligence thus is different qualitatively from what it will be later – it is not judgment or reasoning, but rather sensorimotor processing. Intelligence in this stage is characterized by grasping objects, playing with them, and figuring out simply what the world is like. Infants respond in reflexive ways to the environment, but the reflexes start to be modified to fit environmental requirements.

Probably the two most critical mental accomplishments of this stage are the development of object permanence and of representational thought. Object permanence refers to the notion that an object continues to exist even when it is not immediately visible but rather is out of sight, perhaps because it is hidden behind something else or because it is in a dark room. Representational thought refers to the construction of ways of understanding the world in one's head – for example, through a linguistic representation (a cat is a kind of animal) or a visual representation (what a cat looks like).

The *preoperational stage* occurs roughly between age 2 and age 7. In this stage, children actively develop the mental representations that began to form during the sensorimotor stage. Children start to use words more and more to represent concrete objects. The communication of preoperational children is largely egocentric. It is centered on the self, and the world is perceived from the child's point of view. For example, the child does not understand that another person looking at an object from a different viewpoint will see something different from what the child sees. In conversations, the child often does not take well into account what other people say; rather, the child speaks egocentrically about what is on their mind, regardless of what other people may be thinking.

In the *concrete operational stage*, occurring roughly between 7 and 12 years of age, children become able to mentally manipulate the internal representations they began to create in the preoperational stage. The children now can reason logically, so long as the reasoning applies to concrete objects.

In this stage, children develop various kinds of *conservation*, such as of liquid and mass. They realize that if a liquid is poured from a short, fat beaker into a tall, thin beaker, the latter beaker still contains the same amount of liquid as the former beaker contains. In the preoperational stage, they would have thought the amounts of liquid were different. Or, if a ball of clay that is thin and long is squeezed into more compact and spherical mass, the children will realize that the amount of mass is the same, regardless of how tightly it is packed. During this stage, thinking also becomes reversible, meaning that children can think not only from the beginning to the end or solution of a problem, but also back from the solution to the initial problem.

In the last, *formal operational stage*, children become fully able to think logically. This stage begins at age 11 or 12 years. The children now can think abstractly as well as concretely. For example, if given the numbers 1, 2, 3, 4, they can produce all possible permutations of the numbers by writing down the numbers in a logically sensible order rather than more or less at random. They also now can think more easily of how abstract concepts such as love and hate are both similar to and different from each other.

Piaget's theory was one of the greatest contributions to scholarship in developmental science, but it has not worn well. There are many issues, which are discussed in detail elsewhere. Basically, they are that (a) development is not as stage-like as Piaget made it out to be; (b) Piaget often overestimated the ages at which children first could perform tasks; (c) Piaget often misunderstood the reasons that children failed to solve his tasks successfully; (d) the theory was not as cross-culturally valid as Piaget expected; and (e) some children appear never to have quite reached formal operations as defined by Piaget (Sternberg & Williams, 2010).

Perhaps the greatest challenge with the work of Piaget was his belief that intelligence comprised somewhat separate programs of intellectual development at different ages. Several pioneers in the field of intelligence in infancy, most notably Marc Bornstein, Robert McCall, and Joseph Fagan, have questioned this view (Bornstein & Colombo, 2012; Bornstein, Putnick, & Esposito, 2017; Bornstein & Sigman, 1986; Fagan, Holland, & Wheeler, 2007; Fagan & Singer, 1983; McCall, 1994). In particular, they recognized that there are stunning stabilities in the nature of intelligence from infancy to adulthood.

Bornstein, for example, recognized the importance of infant habituation. Habituation is the rate at which an individual exposed to a stimulus gets used to it, gets bored, and moves on. Infants who later will prove to be more intelligent habituate faster – they get used to a stimulus more quickly and move on. Fagan realized that recognition memory is important to infant intelligence – recognizing a stimulus as having been seen before. A common link in their work was the appreciation that stability in intelligence appeared to stem from infants' ability to cope with novelty. Smarter infants get used to novelty more quickly than do less-smart infants. For the smarter ones, things become familiar (non-novel) rapidly. In short, there is not complete stability in development of intelligence, but there is much more than investigators once thought (Gelman & DeJesus, 2020).

The ground-breaking work of these and other investigators showed why early infant intelligence tests, based on sensory and motor skills, were poor predictors of later intelligence. Essentially, early testers were measuring the wrong thing (Bornstein, 2020). Fluid intelligence is based on coping with novelty. Infant intelligence is no different. It just remained for investigators to recognize this and to figure out a way to measure it in infants. That is what Bornstein and colleagues did.

7.2.2 Neo-Piagetian Models

Recognizing defects in Piaget's model, some researchers suggested that Piaget's model be modified or somehow reorganized. One neo-Piagetian approach has been to propose alternative stages (Demetriou, 1988, 2000; Fischer, 1980; Fischer & Rose, 1994). For example, Kurt Fischer distinguished between typical and optimal levels of performance. The typical level of performance is that level at which an individual usually operates in his or her daily life. The optimal level is the very highest level of performance that an individual is capable of reaching. Fischer emphasized that just because an individual was able, say, to think formal-operationally, it did not mean that they would do so in their daily life. We often see people performing sub-optimally – such as when they think emotionally when they should think logically. For example, they may know, during the time of COVID-19, that they should wear a mask in public, but they do not do it. In Fischer's theory, they are performing at a typical rather than an optimal level.

Another approach has been to propose stages of intellectual development beyond Piaget's stage of formal operations. For example, one such view is that there is a fifth stage – namely, problem finding (Arlin, 1975). Not all people reach this stage. On this view, some people recognize that much of life is not about solving problems that are given to them but, rather, about finding the problems that are most important to solve. In science, for example, much of what distinguishes greater from lesser scientists is that the greater scientists solve more important problems and the lesser scientists solve problems of lesser importance (Zuckerman, 1983). The same is true in the arts: Artists whose work is judged to be of greater importance find more important problems to solve in their artwork (Csikszentmihalyi, 1988, 1996). In everyday life, we are presented with innumerable problems. Some of them work themselves out. We need to find the ones that are actually worth our time to solve.

Although this stage was proposed as following formal operations, children also need to find the problems that are worth their time to solve. For example, they need to distinguish between when they are having a serious problem with another child – as when confronted by a bully – and when they just had a minor disagreement with a friend that likely will work itself out. I have had five children and know that one of the things I have had to teach them is which problems are worth investing effort into solving and which problems are minor and are not worth much effort. So, problem finding really applies at any level.

Another neo-Piagetian view is that there is a different fifth stage: that of so-called dialectical thinking (Labouvie-Vief, 1980). On this point of view, the fifth stage involves understanding other points of view besides one's own and then finding some kind of reconciliation between points of view that at first seem contradictory. People often create false dichotomies. For example, they may believe that either you are a liberal or a conservative; or that either you are in favor of abortion (so-called "pro-choice") or against abortion (so-called "right to life"). Dialectical thinkers realize that many things in life are not cut-and-dried, black-or-white. For example, one might be liberal on domestic policy but conservative on foreign policy; one might be pro-death-penalty for some kinds of issues (e.g., murder committed when a killer tortures a victim) but against the death penalty for other crimes (e.g., murder committed in cold blood but without torture). Dialectical thinkers view issues more complexly than do more simplistic thinkers – they realize that some-times even seemingly opposing points of view can be reconciled (Sternberg, 1998c, 1999a).

Piaget viewed intellectual development as occurring from the inside–outward – that is, people are born with a genetic program that unfolds as the individual matures. In this maturational view, what happens in a child's life does not matter a whole lot: Unless one grows up in a strikingly awful environment, the program will unfold with time because that is what it is preprogrammed to do. A different view would be from the outside-inward.

7.2.3 Vygotsky's Sociocultural Theory of Intellectual Development

Lev Vygotsky, a Russian psychologist, had largely the opposite point of view: that intellectual development unfolds from the outside–inward (Vygotsky, 1962, 1978). Vygotsky believed that a person's mental processes have their origins in their interactions with others. For example, children observe interactions between others; they interact with others themselves; and they use these interactions to facilitate their own development. Essentially, children *internalize* what they observe in their environment. They make into their own other people's patterns of interactions with the environment. Parents are therefore particularly important to children because the way the parents interact toward each other and toward others will be internalized and become part of their children's patterns of behavior. According to Vygotsky, language development is what most helps us internalize complex ideas.

Vygotsky's second major idea beyond internalization is what has come to be called the *zone of proximal development* (ZPD). The ZPD is the difference between a child's level of independent performance – what the child can do on his or her own – and the level of performance the child can reach with guidance from an adult or other expert. The ZPD is viewed as representing the difference between where a child currently is intellectually and where the child can be in the proximate future with appropriate guidance.

A whole method of assessing children's intellectual abilities arose out of Vygotsky's work. It is called dynamic testing or, more broadly, dynamic assessment (Brown & Ferrara, 1985; Grigorenko & Sternberg, 1998; Sternberg & Grigorenko, 2001, 2002). *Dynamic testing* involves some kind of feedback during the administration of an intelligence test. Instead of just giving a child (or adult) a test and then obtaining a result (which is called *static testing*), children get feedback, either after they have solved one problem or after solving several problems. The test measures the child's ability to profit from the feedback they are given. This kind of testing can be especially useful for children whose opportunities to learn have not been comparable to those of other children, such that they come into the testing situation disadvantaged from the very start (Feuerstein, 1979; Lidz, 1991).

Children tested dynamically can often reveal abilities that otherwise would be hidden if they only were tested in a static way (Sternberg, Grigorenko, et al., 2002). If we want to understand children's abilities in a comprehensive way, we need to take more steps to equalize the differences in background with which they enter the testing environment.

So, we have seen that development can help us understand aspects of intelligence that are not easily visible only in people of a given age. Developmental accounts tell us something about both quantitative and qualitative aspects of development. What are the main conclusions we can reach about intelligence as they generalize across ages, not only from the developmental approach, but from all the approaches we have considered?

8 Conclusions about Intelligence and Its Development

In this Element, I have given a brief tour of the theory and research on the nature of human intelligence and its development. When one reads a book, there are always a lot of points to remember and it all can become mixed up together. What are the key take-away messages of this Element? Here are what I believe are the top ten:

1. *Intelligence is, beyond all, the ability broadly to adapt to the environment.* Somehow, this basic necessary feature of intelligence has gotten lost in our preoccupation with measuring intelligence rather than asking what it is we are measuring. If someone scores well on intelligence and proxy tests, but fails to adapt to the environment – for example, acts in ways that lead him or her to be unable to succeed in or even hold a job, or to keep a family functional, or to contribute meaningfully to society – then that someone may be "test-smart," but may not be intelligent in the true sense of adapting to the environment. I have introduced the concept of adaptive intelligence to emphasize that if humans act in ways that hasten the collective demise of humanity, it is hard to see in what sense they are intelligent other than to advance themselves individually at the expense of others, in the present generations and in future generations.

2. *Intelligence is not just what intelligence tests and their proxies test.* Some modern theories, such as those of Howard Gardner and my own, view intelligence quite a bit more broadly than do conventional psychometric theories. But even conventional psychometric theories are broader than the tests. The widely accepted CHC (Cattell–Horn–Carroll) psychometric theory includes a number of abilities that are scarcely measured by conventional tests, such as deductive reasoning (part of fluid intelligence), visual-spatial processing, auditory processing, learning efficiency, working-memory capacity, and motor skills that many contemporary tests do not assess – or, at least, do not assess adequately. And the tests do not assess the creative, practical, and wisdom-based skills of the theory of successful intelligence, or the musical, interpersonal, intrapersonal, bodily-kinesthetic, and naturalist intelligences of Gardner's theory of multiple intelligences. Nor do they measure emotional or social intelligence. Thus,

almost all of the current theories include more – often quite a bit more – than the tests.

3. *Intelligence is not well assessed by a single number, or even two or three numbers.* It is tempting summarize intelligence with a single number, such as an IQ or a couple of SAT scores or composite ACT score, or whatever. But a single number does not do justice to intelligence. Perhaps it would if one believed that all there is to intelligence is general intelligence, or *g*. But, as pointed out in (1) in this list, there is more to intelligence than just a single general ability. For example, someone could be very adept in verbal skills but poor in spatial skills, or vice versa. Some analytically intelligent people are not very creative or lack practical intelligence (common sense). And there are so many high-IQ people who are utterly lacking in wisdom-related skills. As an analogy, you could characterize a person's baseball skills in terms of one number, such as batting average, but that number would not take into account their skills in the infield or outfield, their skills of team play or sportsmanship, or their skills in stealing bases. One number just doesn't cut it.

4. *Intelligence is modifiable.* We know from the Flynn effect that IQs have changed dramatically over generations. They go up, and they go down, presumably in part in response to the demands of the environment in terms of the kinds of skills IQ tests measure. We also know that it is possible achieve at least some meaningful change in broad intellectual skills (Detterman & Sternberg, 1982; Sternberg, Kaufman, & Grigorenko, 2008). We do not now have means of effecting large, lasting increases in intellectual skills. But, as Stephen Ceci (1996) has pointed out, just going to any reasonable kind of school increases one's intellectual skills. If you want to increase your intelligence, there is no magic – learn, think, reason, reflectively solve problems!

5. *Schools often do not teach in ways that optimize the development of a broad range of intellectual skills and attitudes.* Schools in many parts of the world teach to tests. But as we have seen in this Element, those tests tend to sample only a narrow portion of intelligence. Hence, emphasizing largely memory and some analysis will not fully teach children to think intelligently. Children also need to be taught in ways that develop their creative, practical, and wisdom-based skills.

6. *Requirements for being intelligent vary across time, cultures, and subcultures.* There are certain mental processes that are needed to be intelligent in virtually any culture, such as recognizing the existence of problems, defining the problems, setting up strategies for solving the problems, and monitoring one's problem solving (Sternberg, 2007, 2012). But the ways

these processes play out differ widely across time and space. For example, the adaptive skills needed to prevent transmission of disease spread through airborne droplets has greatly increased in a matter of months. What is smart can change over generations, or from one day to the next.

7. *Folk theories of intelligence also vary across time and space.* Folk theories are our implicit theories of what we believe intelligence to be. They are the theories of laypeople. They matter – a lot – because most judgments of intelligence are based not on test scores, but on informal or formal personal interactions. To appear to be smart in a milieu, you need to understand the folk theory of intelligence of the people you are dealing with.

8. *Intelligence is to be found in the interaction between biology and environment.* Contrary to what some theorists believe, intelligence does not reside solely in the brain (Haier, 2016). Rather, it is in the interaction between the brain and the environment. The environment is influential in specifying what constitutes intelligence in a given context. Moreover, even genes interact with the environment through epigenetic influences (environmental influences that turn genes on and off). Just studying brains will never tell us the whole story as to what intelligence is. And for everyday decisions, such as whether to buy a particular car or house, or to marry a particular person, analyzing the brain will be insufficient for understanding the contextual forces that can make one or another decision "intelligent."

9. *The development of intelligence is largely, although not fully continuous.* Studies of children's ways of coping with novelty have shown that intelligence develops in ways that are at least in part continuous. If you want to promote intelligence in a child, you might want to promote the skills involved in coping with novel situations. In later years, there can be discontinuity as brain diseases affect some people in ways that might not have been predictable. But many individuals preserve high levels of mental functioning, especially those relevant in their careers, until later in life.

10. *Social policies aimed at preserving the socioeconomic status quo ill serve any society that wants optimally to develop the intelligence of its citizens.* There are many forces in societies that seek to preserve the status quo – to keep those who are "on top" on top, and those who are "at the bottom" at the bottom. For example, university admissions often favor the wealthy, and the quality of schools in a given neighborhood may reflect the wealth of the adults of that neighborhood, transmitting privilege (or the lack thereof) between generations. If we want all children and adults to optimize their intelligence, we have to find ways to allow them to flourish, not

to become trapped in a societal system that determines their places with little or no regard to their broad intellectual potential. If humanity wishes to have a future, it must provide more equitable opportunities for all optimally to develop their intelligence, not just those born into positions of privilege.

References

Arlin, P. K. (1975). Cognitive development in adulthood: A fifth stage? *Developmental Psychology, 11*(5), 602–606. https://doi.org/10.1037/0012-1649.11.5.602

Azuma, H., & Kashiwagi, K. (1987). Descriptions for an intelligent person: A Japanese study. *Japanese Psychological Research, 29*(1), 17–26.

Bardon, A. (2019). *The truth about denial: Bias and self-deception in science, politics, and religion.* Oxford University Press.

Binet, A., & Simon, T. (1916), *The development of intelligence in children* (E. S. Kite, trans). Williams & Wilkins.

Boring, E. G. (1923). Intelligence as the tests measure it. *New Republic, 36*, 35–37.

Bornstein, M. H. (2020). Intelligence in infancy. In R. J. Sternberg (Ed.), *Cambridge handbook of intelligence* (2nd ed., pp. 124–154). Cambridge University Press.

Bornstein, M. H., & Colombo, J. (2012). Infant cognitive functioning and mental development. In S. Pauen (Ed.), *Early childhood development and later achievement* (pp. 118–147). Cambridge University Press.

Bornstein, M. H., & Putnick, D. L. (2019). *The architecture of the child mind.* Routledge.

Bornstein, M. H., & Sigman, M. D. (1986). Continuity in mental development from infancy. *Child Development, 57*(2), 251–274.

Bornstein, M. H., Putnick, D. L., & Esposito, G. (2017). Continuity and stability in development. *Child Development Perspectives, 11*(2), 113–1199.

Bronfenbrenner, U. (2009). *The ecology of human development: Experiments by nature and design.* Harvard University Press.

Brown, A. L., & Ferrara, R. A. (1985). Diagnosing zones of proximal development. In J. V. Wertsch (Ed.). *Culture, communication, and cognition: Vygotskian perspectives* (pp. 273–305). Cambridge University Press.

Carroll, J. B. (1993). *Human cognitive abilities: A survey of factor-analytic studies.* Cambridge University Press.

Cattell, R. B. (1987). *Beyondism: Religion from science.* Praeger.

Ceci, S. J. (1996). *On intelligence: A bioecological treatise on intellectual development* (expanded ed.). Harvard University Press.

Ceci, S. J., & Bronfenbrenner, U. (1985). "Don't forget to take the cupcakes out of the oven": Prospective memory, strategic time-monitoring, and context. *Child Development, 56*(1), 152–164. https://doi.org/10.2307/1130182

Ceci, S. J., & Roazzi, A. (1994). The effects of context on cognition: Postcards from Brazil. In R. J. Sternberg & R. K. Wagner (Eds.), *Mind in context: Interactionist perspectives on human intelligence* (pp. 74–101). Cambridge University Press.

Chappell, B. (2020, May 21). US could have saved 36,000 lives if social distancing started 1 week earlier: study. *NPR*, www.npr.org/sections/corona virus-live-updates/2020/05/21/860077940/u-s-could-have-saved-36–000-lives-if-social-distancing-started-1-week-earlier-st

Csikszentmihalyi, M. (1988). Society, culture, and person: A systems view of creativity. In R. J. Sternberg (Ed.), *The nature of creativity* (pp. 325–339). Cambridge University Press.

Csikszentmihalyi, M. (1996). *Creativity: Flow and the psychology of discovery and invention.* HarperCollins.

Dasen, P. (1984). The cross-cultural study of intelligence: Piaget and the Baoule. *International Journal of Psychology, 19*(4–5), 407–434.

Deary, I. J., Whalley, L. J., & Starr, J. M. (2009). *A lifetime of intelligence: Follow-up studies of the Scottish Mental Surveys of 1932 and 1947.* American Psychological Association.

Deary, I. J., Whiteman, M. C., Starr, J. M., Whalley, L. J., & Fox, H. C. (2004). The impact of childhood intelligence on later life: Following up the Scottish Mental Surveys of 1932 and 1947. *Journal of Personality and Social Psychology, 86*(1), 130–147.

Demetriou, A. (Ed.), (1988). *The neo-Piagetian theories of cognitive development: Toward an integration.* North-Holland.

Demetriou, A., (2000). Organization and development of self-understanding and self-regulation: Toward a general theory. In M. Boekaerts, P. R. Pintrich, & M. Zeidner (Eds.), *Handbook of self-regulation* (pp. 209–251). Academic Press.

Detterman, D. K., & Sternberg, R. J. (Eds.). (1982). *How and how much can intelligence be increased?* Ablex.

Ellingsen, V. J., & Engle, R. W. (2020). Cognitive approaches to intelligence. In R. J. Sternberg (Ed.), *Human intelligence: An introduction* (pp. 104–138). Cambridge University Press.

Ellis, B. J., Abrams, L. S., Masten, A. S., Sternberg, R. J., Tottenham, N., & Frankenhuis, W. E. (2020). Hidden talents in harsh environments. *Development and Psychopathology* 1–19, https://doi.org/10.1017/S0954579420000887.

Engle, R. W, & Kane, M. J. (2004). Executive attention, working memory capacity, and a two-factor theory of cognitive control. In B. H. Ross (Ed.), *The psychology of learning and motivation* (Vol. 44, pp. 145–199). Academic Press.

Ericsson, A. & Poole, R. (2017). *Peak: Secrets from the new science of expertise.* Eamon/Dolan/Houghton Mifflin Harcourt.

Fagan, J. F., Holland, C. R., & Wheeler, K. (2007). The prediction, from infancy, of adult IQ and achievement. *Intelligence, 35*(3), 225–231.

Fagan, J. F., & Singer, L T. (1983). Infant recognition memory as a measure of intelligence. In L. P. Lipsitt (Ed.), *Advances in infancy research* (Vol. 2, pp. 31–79). Ablex Publishers.

Faulkner, W. (2012). *Requiem for a nun.* Vintage.

Feuerstein, R. (1979). *The dynamic assessment of retarded performers: The Learning Potential Assessment Device theory, instruments, and techniques.* University Park Press.

Fischer, K. W. (1980). A theory of cognitive development: The control and construction of hierarchies of skills. *Psychological Review, 87*(6), 477–531.

Fischer, K. W., & Rose, S. P. (1994). Dynamic development of coordination of components in brain and behavior: A framework for theory and research. In G. Dawson & K. W. Fischer (Eds.), *Human behavior and the developing brain* (pp. 3–66). Guilford Press.

Flynn, J. R. (1987). Massive IQ gains in 14 nations. *Psychological Bulletin, 101*(2), 171–191.

Flynn, R. J. (2012). *Are we getting smarter?* Cambridge University Press.

Flynn, J. R. (2016). *Does your family make you smarter? Nature, nurture, and human autonomy.* Cambridge University Press.

Frensch, P. A., & Sternberg, R. J. (1989). Expertise and intelligent thinking: When is it worse to know better? In R. J. Sternberg (Ed.), *Advances in the psychology of human intelligence* (Vol. 5, pp. 157–188). Lawrence Erlbaum Associates.

Frey, M. C., & Detterman. D. K. (2004). Scholastic assessment or *g?* The relationship between the Scholastic Assessment Test and general cognitive ability. *Psychological Science, 15*(6), 373–378.

Galton, F. (1869/1892/1962). *Hereditary genius: An inquiry into its laws and consequences.* Macmillan/Fontana.

Galton, F. (1883/1907/1973). *Inquiries into human faculty and its development.* AMS Press

Gardner, H. (1983). *Frames of mind: The theory of multiple intelligences.* Basic Books.

Gardner, H. (2011). *Frames of mind: The theory of multiple intelligences* (rev. ed.). Basic Books.

Garrett, B. (2020, May 3). We should all be preppers. *The Atlantic,* www.theatlantic.com/ideas/archive/2020/05/we-should-all-be-preppers/611074/

Gelman, S. A., & DeJesus, J. M. (2020). Intelligence in childhood. In R. J. Sternberg (Ed.), *Cambridge handbook of intelligence* (2nd ed., pp. 155–180). Cambridge University Press.

Goldberg, M. (2020, June 22). America is too broken to fight the coronavirus. *New York Times*, www.nytimes.com/2020/06/22/opinion/us-coronavirus-trump.html?action=click&module=Opinion&pgtype=Homepage.

Gould, S. J. (1981). *The mismeasure of man*. W. W. Norton.

Greenfield, P. M. (2020). Historical evolution of intelligence. In R. J. Sternberg (Ed.), *Cambridge handbook of intelligence* (2nd ed., pp. 916–939). Cambridge University Press.

Grigorenko, E. L., & Sternberg, R. J. (1998). Dynamic testing. *Psychological Bulletin, 124*, 75–111.

Grigorenko, E. L., & Sternberg, R. J. (2001). Analytical, creative, and practical intelligence as predictors of self-reported adaptive functioning: A case study in Russia. *Intelligence, 29*, 57–73.

Grigorenko, E. L., Meier, E., Lipka, J., Mohatt, G., Yanez, E., & Sternberg, R. J. (2004). Academic and practical intelligence: A case study of the Yup'ik in Alaska. *Learning and Individual Differences, 14*, 183–207.

Grigorenko, E. L., Ruzgis, P., & Sternberg, R. J. (Eds.) (1997). *Psychology in Russia: Past, present, future*. Nova Science.

Guilford, J. P. (1967). *The nature of human intelligence*. McGraw-Hill.

Guilford, J. P. (1988). Some changes in the structure-of-intellect model. *Educational and Psychological Measurement, 48*, 1–4.

Haier, R. J. (2016). *The neuroscience of intelligence*. Cambridge University Press.

Haier, R. J. (2020). Biological approaches to intelligence. In R. J. Sternberg (Ed.), *Human intelligence: An introduction* (pp. 139–173). Cambridge University Press.

Haier, R. J., Karama, S., Leyba, L., & Jung, R. E. (2009). MRI assessment of cortical thickness and functional activity changes in adolescent girls following three months of practice on a visual-spatial task. *BMC Research Notes, 2*, 174. http://doi.org/10.1186/1756-0500-2-174.

Haier, R. J., Siegel, B. V., Nuechterlein, K. H., Hazlett, E., Wu, J. C., Paek, J., ... & Buchsbaum, M. S. (1988). Cortical glucose metabolic-rate correlates of abstract reasoning and attention studies with positron emission tomography. *Intelligence, 12*(2), 199–217.

Haier, R. J., Siegel, B. V., Tang, C., Abel, L., & Buchsbaum, M. S. (1992). Intelligence and changes in regional cerebral glucose metabolic rate following learning. *Intelligence, 16(3–4)*, 415–426. https://doi.org/10.1016/0160-2896(92)90018-M.

Hall, S. (2015, October 26). Exxon knew about climate change almost 40 years ago. *Scientific American*, www.scientificamerican.com/article/exxon-knew-about-climate-change-almost-40-years-ago/

Hedlund, J. (2020). Practical intelligence. In R. J. Sternberg (Ed.), *Cambridge handbook of intelligence* (2nd ed., pp. 736–755). Cambridge University Press.

Henig, R. M. (2020, April 8). Experts warned of a pandemic decades ago. Why weren't we ready? *National Geographic*, www.nationalgeographic.com/science/2020/04/experts-warned-pandemic-decades-ago-why-not-ready-for-coronavirus/#close

Herrnstein, R. J., & Murray, C. (1994). *The bell curve*. Free Press.

Hertzog, C. (2020a). Intelligence in adulthood. In R. J. Sternberg (Ed.), *Cambridge handbook of intelligence* (2nd ed., pp. 181–204). Cambridge University Press.

Hertzog, C. (2020b). Lifespan development of intelligence. In R. J. Sternberg (Ed.), *Human intelligence: An introduction* (2nd ed., pp. 279–313). Cambridge University Press.

Hilt, P. J. (1997, August 15). Racism accusations and award is delayed. *New York Times*, www.nytimes.com/1997/08/15/us/racism-accusations-and-award-is-delayed.html

Horn, J. L., & Knapp. J. R. (1973). On the subjective character of the empirical base of Guilford's structure-of-intellect model. *Psychological Bulletin, 80*, 33–43.

Hughes, V. (2014, March 5). Epigenetics: The sins of the father. *Nature, 507*, www.nature.com/news/epigenetics-the-sins-of-the-father-1.14816

Hunt, E. B., Lunneborg, C., & Lewis, J. (1975). What does it mean to be high verbal? *Cognitive Psychology, 7*, 194–227.

"Intelligence and its measurement": A symposium (1921). *Journal of Educational Psychology*, 12, 123–147, 195–216, 271–275.

Jensen, A. R. (1998). *The g factor*. Praeger-Greenwood.

Jung, R. E., & Haier, R. J. (2007). The parieto-frontal integration theory (P-FIT) of intelligence: Converging neuroimaging evidence. *Behavioral and Brain Sciences, 30*(2), 135–154.

Kaufman, A. S., Schneider, W. J., & Kaufman, J. C. (2020). Psychometric approaches to studying intelligence. In R. J. Sternberg (Ed.), *Human intelligence: An introduction* (pp. 67–103). Cambridge University Press.

Knopik, V. S., Neiderhiser, J. M., DeFries, J. M., & Plomin, R. (2016). *Behavioral genetics* (7th ed.). Worth.

Koenig, K.A., Frey, M.C. & Detterman, D.K. (2008). ACT and general cognitive ability. *Intelligence, 36*, 153–160.

Kuhn, T. S. (2012). *The structure of scientific revolutions* (50th anniversary ed.). University of Chicago Press.

Labouvie-Vief, G. (1980). Beyond formal operations: Uses and limits of pure logic in life-span development. *Human Development, 23,* 141–161.

Lave, J. (1988) *Cognition in practice.* Cambridge University Press.

Lidz, C. S. (1991). *Practitioner's guide to dynamic assessment.* Guilford Press.

Locke, S. F. (2008, September 11). Was the dinosaurs' long reign on Earth a fluke? *Scientific American,* www.scientificamerican.com/article/was-the-dinosaurs-long-reign-a-fluke/

Lutz, C. (1985). Ethnopsychology compared to what? Explaining behaviour and consciousness among the Ifaluk. In G. M. White & J. Kirkpatrick (Eds.), *Person, self, and experience: Exploring Pacific ethnopsychologies* (pp. 35–79). University of California Press.

Maguire, E. A., Gadian, D. G., Johnsrude, I. S., Good, C. D., Ashburner, J., Frackowiak, R. S. J., & Frith, C. D. (2000). Navigation-related structural change in the hippocampi of taxi drivers. *PNAS, 97*(8), 4398–4403, https://doi.org/10.1073/pnas.070039597

Malone, T. W., & Woolley, A. W. (2020). Collective intelligence. In R. J. Sternberg (Ed.), *Cambridge handbook of intelligence* (2nd ed., pp. 780–801). Cambridge University Press.

Markus, H. R., & Conner, A. (2014). *Clash: How to thrive in a multicultural world.* Plume.

Marquie, J. C., Duarte, L. R., Bessieres, P., Dalm, C., Gentil, C., & Ruidavets, J. B. (2010). Higher mental stimulation at work is associated with improved cognitive functioning in both young and older workers. *Ergonomics, 53*(11), 1287–1301. http://doi.org/10.1080/00140139.2010.519125.

McCall, R. B. (1994). What process mediates prediction of childhood IQ from infant habituation and recognition memory? Speculations on the roles of inhibition and rate of information processing. *Intelligence, 18,* 107–125.

McCarthy, C. (2007). *The road.* Vintage.

McGrew, K. S. (2005). The Cattell-Horn-Carroll theory of cognitive abilities: Past, present, and future. In D. P. Flanagan & P. L. Harrison (Eds.), *Contemporary intellectual assessment: Theories, tests, issues* (2nd ed. pp. 136–181). Guilford Press.

Moreno, J. E. (2020, June 20). Most Trump rally attendees opt not to wear face masks. *The Hill,* https://thehill.com/homenews/campaign/503752-most-trump-rally-attendees-opt-not-to-wear-face-masks

Murray, C. (2020). *Human diversity: The biology gender, race, and class.* Twelve.

Nuñes, T. (1994). Street intelligence. In R. J. Sternberg (Ed.), *Encyclopedia of human intelligence* (Vol. 2, pp. 1045–1049). Macmillan.

Okagaki, L., & Sternberg, R. J. (1993). Parental beliefs and children's school performance. *Child Development, 64*(1), 36–56.

Piaget, J. (1972). *The psychology of intelligence.* Littlefield Adams.

Plomin, R., DeFries, J. C., Knopik, V. S., & Neiderhiser, J. M. (2013). *Behavioral genetics* (6th ed.). Worth.

Poole, F. J. P. (1985). Coming into social being: Cultural images of infants in Bimin-Kuskusmin folk psychology. In G. M. White & J. Kirkpatrick (Eds.). *Person, self, and experience: Exploring Pacific ethnopsychologies* (pp. 183–244). University of California Press.

Ruzgis, P. M & Grigorenko, E. L. (1994). Cultural meaning systems, intelligence and personality. In R. J. Sternberg and P. Ruzgis (Eds.). *Personality and intelligence* (pp. 248–270). Cambridge University Press.

Sackett, P. R., Shewach, O. R., & Dahlke, J. A. (2020). The predictive value of general intelligence. In R. J. Sternberg (Ed.), *Human intelligence: An introduction* (pp. 381–414). New York: Cambridge University Press.

Salthouse, T. A. (2006). Mental exercises and mental aging: Evaluating the validity of the "use it or lose it" hypothesis. *Perspectives on Psychological Science, 1*, 68–87.

Schliemann, A. D., & Magalhües, V. P. (1990). *Proportional reasoning: From shops, to kitchens, laboratories, and, hopefully, schools.* Proceedings of the Fourteenth International Conference for the Psychology of Mathematics Education, Oaxtepec, Mexico.

Schooler, C., & Kaplan, L. J. (2009). How those who have, thrive: Mechanisms underlying the well-being of the advantaged later in life. In H. B. Bosworth & C. Hertzog (Eds.), *Aging and cognition: Research methodologies and empirical advantages* (pp. 121–141). American Psychological Association.

Serpell, R. (1996). Cultural models of childhood in indigenous socialization and formal schooling in Zambia. In C. P. Hwang & M. E. Lamb (Eds), *Images of childhood.* (pp. 129–142). Lawrence Erlbaum.

Serpell, R. (2002). The embeddedness of human development within sociocultural context: Pedagogical, and political implications. *Social Development, 11*(2) 290–295.

Simberloff, D. (N.D.) A modern mass extinction? *PBS: Evolution.* www .pbs.org/wgbh/evolution/extinction/massext/statement_03.html

Smithsonian Institution (2018, September 14). Survival of the adaptable: What does it mean to be human? https://humanorigins.si.edu/research/climate-and-human-evolution/survival-adaptable

Spearman, C. (1904). "General intelligence," objectively determined and measured. *American Journal of Psychology, 15*(2), 201–292.

Spearman, C. (1927). *The abilities of man*. Macmillan.

Sternberg, R. J. (1977a). Component processes in analogical reasoning. *Psychological Review, 84*, 353–378.

Sternberg, R. J. (1977b). *Intelligence, information processing, and analogical reasoning: The componential analysis of human abilities*. Lawrence Erlbaum Associates.

Sternberg, R. J. (1983). Components of human intelligence. *Cognition, 15*, 1–48.

Sternberg, R. J (1990). *Metaphors of mind*. Cambridge University Press.

Sternberg, R. J. (1997). *Successful intelligence*. Plume.

Sternberg, R. J. (1998a). Abilities are forms of developing expertise. *Educational Researcher, 27*(3), 11–20.

Sternberg, R. J. (1998b). *Cupid's arrow: The course of love through time*. Cambridge University Press.

Sternberg, R. J. (1998c). The dialectic as a tool for teaching psychology. *Teaching of Psychology, 25*, 177–180.

Sternberg, R. J. (1998d). Principles of teaching for successful intelligence. *Educational Psychologist, 33*, 65–72.

Sternberg, R. J. (1999a). A dialectical basis for understanding the study of cognition. In R. J. Sternberg (Ed.), *The nature of cognition* (pp. 51–78). The MIT Press.

Sternberg, R. J. (1999b). Intelligence as developing expertise. *Contemporary Educational Psychology, 24*, 359–375.

Sternberg, R. J. (1999c). A propulsion model of types of creative contributions. *Review of General Psychology, 3*, 83–100.

Sternberg, R. J. (2003). *Wisdom, intelligence, and creativity synthesized*. Cambridge University Press.

Sternberg, R. J. (2004). Culture and intelligence. *American Psychologist, 59*(5), 325–338.

Sternberg, R. J. (2007). Intelligence and culture. In S. Kitayama & D. Cohen (Eds.), *Hand of cultural psychology* (pp. 547–568). Guilford Press.

Sternberg, R. J. (2010). *College admissions for the 21st century*. Harvard University Press.

Sternberg, R. J. (2012). Intelligence in its cultural context. In M. Gelfand, C.-Y. Chiu, and Y.-Y. Hong (Eds.), *Advances in cultures and psychology* (Vol. 2, pp. 205–248). Oxford University Press.

Sternberg, R. J. (2013). Teaching for wisdom. In S. David, I. Boniwell, & A. C. Ayers (Eds.), *Oxford handbook of happiness* (pp. 631–643). Oxford University Press.

Sternberg, R. J. (2016). *What universities can be: A new model for preparing students for active concerned citizenship and ethical leadership.* Cornell University Press.

Sternberg, R. J. (2017). ACCEL: A new model for identifying the gifted. *Roeper Review, 39* (3), 139–152. www.tandfonline.com/eprint/kSvRMFf9R8tAJPDRf XrJ/full.

Sternberg, R. J. (2019a). Introduction to the Cambridge Handbook of Wisdom: Race to Samarra: The critical importance of wisdom in the world today. In R. J. Sternberg & J. Glueck (Eds.), *Cambridge handbook of wisdom* (pp. 3–9). Cambridge University Press.

Sternberg, R. J. (2019b). Is gifted education on the right path? The ACCEL model of giftedness. In D. Sisk, B. Wallace, & J. Senior (Eds.), *Hand of gifted education* (pp. 5–18). Sage.

Sternberg, R. J. (2019c). A theory of adaptive intelligence and its relation to general intelligence. *Journal of Intelligence,* https://doi.org/10.3390/jintelligence7040023.

Sternberg, R. J. (Ed.) (2020). *Cambridge handbook of intelligence* (2nd ed.). Cambridge University Press.

Sternberg, R. J. (in press). *Adaptive intelligence.* Cambridge University Press.

Sternberg, R. J., & Davidson, J. E. (1999). Insight. In M. Runco & S. R. Pritzker (Eds.), *Encyclopedia of creativity* (Vol. 2, pp. 57–69). Academic Press.

Sternberg, R. J., & Grigorenko, E. L. (2001). All testing is dynamic testing. *Issues in Education, 7*(2), 137–170.

Sternberg, R. J., & Grigorenko, E. L. (2002). *Dynamic testing.* Cambridge University Press.

Sternberg, R. J., & Grigorenko, E. L. (2007). *Teaching for successful intelligence* (2nd ed.). Corwin Press.

Sternberg, R. J., & Hedlund, J. (2002). Practical intelligence, g, and work psychology. *Human Performance, 15*(1/2), 143–160.

Sternberg, R. J., & Suben, J. (1986). The socialization of intelligence. In M. Perlmutter (Ed.), *Perspectives on intellectual development: Vol. 19. Minnesota symposia on child psychology* (pp. 201–235). Lawrence Erlbaum Associates.

Sternberg, R. J., & The Rainbow Project Collaborators (2006). The Rainbow Project: Enhancing the SAT through assessments of analytical, practical and creative skills. *Intelligence, 34*(4), 321–350.

Sternberg, R. J., & Williams, W. M. (2010). *Educational psychology* (2nd ed.). Pearson/Merrill.

Sternberg, R. J., Bonney, C. R., Gabora, L, & Merrifield, M. (2012). WICS: A model for college and university admissions. *Educational Psychologist*, 47(1), 30–41.

Sternberg, R. J., Conway, B. E., Ketron, J. L., & Bernstein, M. (1981). People's conceptions of intelligence. *Journal of Personality and Social Psychology*, 41, 37–55.

Sternberg, R. J., Forsythe, G. B., Hedlund, J., Horvath, J., Snook, S., Williams, W. M., Wagner, R. K., & Grigorenko, E. L. (2000). *Practical intelligence in everyday life*. Cambridge University Press.

Sternberg, R. J., Grigorenko, E. L., Ferrari, M., & Clinkenbeard, P. (1999). A triarchic analysis of an aptitude–treatment interaction. *European Journal of Psychological Assessment*, 15(1), 1–11.

Sternberg, R. J., Grigorenko, E. L., & Kidd, K. K. (2005). Intelligence, race, and genetics. *American Psychologist*, 60(1), 46–59.

Sternberg, R. J., Grigorenko, E. L., Ngorosho, D., Tantufuye, E., Mbise, A., Nokes, C., Jukes, M., & Bundy, D. A. (2002). Assessing intellectual potential in rural Tanzanian school children. *Intelligence*, 30, 141–162.

Sternberg, R. J., Jarvin, L., & Grigorenko, E. L. (2009). *Teaching for wisdom, intelligence, creativity, and success*. Corwin.

Sternberg, R. J., Kaufman, J. C., & Grigorenko, E. L. (2008). *Applied intelligence*. Cambridge University Press.

Sternberg, R. J., Kaufman, J. C., & Pretz, J. E. (2002). *The creativity conundrum: A propulsion model of kinds of creative contributions*. Psychology Press.

Sternberg, R. J., Nokes, K., Geissler, P. W., Prince, R., Okatcha, F., Bundy, D. A., & Grigorenko, E. L. (2001). The relationship between academic and practical intelligence: A case study in Kenya. *Intelligence*, 29, 401–418.

Sternberg, R. J., Wagner, R. K., Williams, W. M., & Horvath, J. A. (1995). Testing common sense. *American Psychologist*, 50(11), 912–927.

Super C.M., & Harkness, S. (1982). The development of affect in infancy and early childhood. In D. Wagner & H. Stevenson (Eds.). *Cultural perspectives on child development* (pp. 1–19). W. H. Freeman.

Super, C. M., & Harkness, S. (1986). The developmental niche: A conceptualization at the interface of child and culture. *International Journal of Behavioral Development*, 9, 545–569.

Super, C. M & Harkness, S. (1993). The developmental niche: A conceptualization at the interface of child and culture. In R. A. Pierce, M. A. Black, (Eds.). *Life-span development: A diversity reader*, (pp. 61–77). Kendall/Hunt Publishing Co.

Thomson, G. H. (1916). A hierarchy without a general factor. *British Journal of Psychology*, 8, 271–281.

Thurstone, L. L. (1938). *Primary mental abilities*. University of Chicago Press.

Times Editorial Board (2020, April 21). *Los Angeles Times*, www.latimes.com/opinion/story/2020-04-21/live-free-or-die-isnt-a-hypothetical-choice-in-a-pandemic

Tucker-Drob, E. M. (2009). *Differentiation of cognitive abilities across the lifespan. Developmental Psychology, 45*(4), 1097–1118. http://doi.org/10.1037/a0015864

Visser, B. A., Ashton, M. C., & Vernon, P. A. (2006). Beyond *g:* Putting multiple intelligence theory of the test. *Intelligence, 34,* 487–502.

Von Stumm, S., & Plomin, R. (2015). Socioeconomic status and the growth of intelligence from infancy through adolescence. *Intelligence, 48,* 30–36. http://doi.org/10.1016/j.intell.2014.10.002.

Vygotsky, L. S. (1962). *Thought and language*. (Original work published 1934). MIT Press.

Vygotsky, L. S. (1978). *Mind in society: The development of higher psychological processes*. Harvard University Press.

Wechsler, D. (1940). Non-intellective factor in general intelligence. *Psychological Bulletin, 37,* 444–445.

Wechsler, D. (1944). *The measurement and appraisal of adult intelligence*. Williams & Wilkins.

Wise, A. (2020, April 15). Trump says the US is past its peak on new coronavirus cases. *NPR*, www.npr.org/2020/04/15/833444593/watch-white-house-holds-briefing-amid-who-governor-spats

Wissler, C. (1901). The correlation of mental and physical tests. *Psychological Review Monograph Supplement, 3*(6), 1–62.

Zuckerman, H. (1983). The scientific elite: Nobel laureates' mutual influences. In R. S. Albert (Ed.), *Genius and eminence: The social psychology of creativity and exceptional achievement* (Vol. 5, pp. 241–252). Pergamon.

Acknowledgment

I would like to acknowledge the late Dr. Gordon H. Bower, my graduate advisor and mentor at Stanford, recently deceased. Gordon was the best mentor one possibly could hope to have, and, after graduate school, remained a lifelong friend. I have been forever grateful to him for supporting my research on intelligence when I was in graduate school despite the fact that the topic was one on which he never did any research. His incredible success as a mentor derived from his willingness to let each of his students follow their dreams, and that is, I believe, what we all did.

Cambridge Elements ≡

Child Development

Marc H. Bornstein
National Institute of Child Health and Human Development, Bethesda
Institute for Fiscal Studies, London
UNICEF, New York City
Marc H. Bornstein is an Affiliate of the Eunice Kennedy Shriver National Institute of Child Health and Human Development, an International Research Fellow at the Institute for Fiscal Studies (London), and UNICEF Senior Advisor for Research for ECD Parenting Programmes. Bornstein is President Emeritus of the Society for Research in Child Development, Editor Emeritus of *Child Development*, and founding Editor of *Parenting: Science and Practice*.

About the Series
Child development is a lively and engaging, yet serious and purposeful subject of academic study that encompasses myriad of theories, methods, substantive areas, and applied concerns. Cambridge Elements in Child Development proposes to address all these key areas, with unique, comprehensive, and state-of-the-art treatments, introducing readers to the primary currents of research and to original perspectives on, or contributions to, principal issues and domains in the field.

Cambridge Elements ≡

Child Development

Elements in the Series

Printed in the United States
By Bookmasters